W9-CHV-642

3 2044 011 148 293

WITHDRAWN

Economic Policy Reform in Developing Countries

The Kuznets Memorial Lectures

Series Editor: T. Paul Schultz

Inequality, Poverty, and History
Jeffrey G. Williamson

Economic Policy Reform in Developing Countries
Anne O. Krueger

WITHDRAWN

Economic Policy Reform in Developing Countries

The Kuznets Memorial Lectures at the Economic Growth Center, Yale University

Anne O. Krueger

BLACKWELL
Oxford UK & Cambridge USA

RECEIVED

APR 2 1993

HC
59.7
.K75 1992
Krueger, Anne O.
Economic policy reform in
developing countries

AMH 5289-1/2

Copyright © Anne O. Krueger 1992

The right of Anne O. Krueger to be identified as author of this work
has been asserted in accordance with the Copyright, Designs and
Patents Act 1988.

First published 1992

Blackwell Publishers
Three Cambridge Center
Cambridge, Massachusetts 02142
USA

108 Cowley Road
Oxford OX4 1JF
UK

All rights reserved. Except for the quotation of short passages for the
purposes of criticism and review, no part may be reproduced, stored in
a retrieval system, or transmitted, in any form or by any means,
electronic, mechanical, photocopying, recording or otherwise, without
the prior permission of the publisher.

Except in the United States of America, this book is sold subject to
the condition that it shall not, by way of trade or otherwise, be lent,
resold, hired out, or otherwise circulated without the publisher's prior
consent in any form of binding or cover other than that in which it is
published and without a similar condition including this condition
being imposed on the subsequent purchaser.

Library of Congress Cataloging in Publication Data
Krueger, Anne O.
Economic policy reform in developing countries: the Kuznets memorial
lectures at the Economic Growth Center, Yale University/Anne O.
Krueger.
p.   cm.
Includes bibliographical references and index.
ISBN   1-55786-274-5
1. Developing countries—economic policy. I. Title.
HC59.7.K75   1992
338.9′009172′4—dc20   91-25959 CIP

British Library Cataloguing in Publication Data
A CIP catalogue record for this book is available from the British
Library.

Typeset in 10½ on 12 pt Baskerville
by Photo·graphics, Honiton, Devon
Printed in Great Britain by Billing & Sons Limited, Worcester

This book is printed on acid-free paper.

RECEIVED

APR 2 1993

Kennedy School
Library

Contents

Preface by Series Editor

In 1986 the Economic Growth Center of Yale University established a lecture series in honor of the late Simon Kuznets, who participated in founding the Center in 1961 and served thereafter on its Executive Committee until his death in 1985. Kuznets received the Nobel Prize in Economics in 1971 for his many contributions to the design of national income accounts and to our understanding of the characteristics of modern economic growth. This Memorial Lecture Series is dedicated to "Quantitative Aspects of the Economic Growth Among Nations," the title Simon Kuznets selected for his pioneering series of ten short monographs that were published by the journal *Economic Development and Cultural Change* from 1956 to 1967.

The lectures have been endowed by the generosity of gifts received from numerous friends and colleagues of Simon Kuznets from many parts of the world, as well as by a contribution from the Economic Growth Center.

The first series of lectures was presented at Yale University in March 1987 by Angus Deaton of Princeton University on "Household Behavior in Developing Countries". In April 1988 Amartya Sen of Harvard University presented the second series of Kuznets Memorial Lectures entitled "Inequality Reexamined". Jeffrey G. Williamson of Harvard University gave the third lectures entitled "Inequality and

Modern Economic Growth: What Does History Tell Us?"
which was published as *Inequality, Poverty, and History* by Basil
Blackwell in 1990. Included here is the fourth set of lectures
presented in April 1990 by Anne O. Krueger of Duke University on "Economic Policy Reform in Developing Countries".

Ms Krueger joined the economics faculty at Duke University as Arts and Sciences Professor after serving as Vice
President for Economics and Research at the World Bank
from 1982 to 1987. During her tenure at the Bank, the largest
economic research organization in the world, the research
agenda at the Bank evolved in new directions, became more
visible to the wider economics community, and more influential as US international assistance diminished under Reagan.
One of her innovations was the initiation of a series of comparative economic studies between countries, addressing
major issues of international economic development with the
goal of distilling new directions for World Bank policy. She
also has experience as a consultant for the US Agency for
International Development, the US Treasury, HIID, NSF,
and other private and multilateral organizations. She has
written many books and journal articles on international
economic policy, problems of international economics and
exchange rate policy, the consequences of protection on the
composition of trade and employment, and seminal papers
on rent-seeking behavior within a restrictive trade regime.

The issue that Professor Krueger addresses in these lectures
is the conditions that set the stage for the "crisis in development" that forced many low income countries during the
1980s to revamp their economic policies. Why did the set of
national economic policies that were adopted by most low
income countries in the decade after the Second World War
as colonialism receded suddenly appear unsustainable in the
early 1980s? What distinguished the successful from the
unsuccessful economic policy reform packages adopted during
this period, and what are the prospects for the reemergence
of economic growth in the countries of Latin America, Africa,
and South Asia, many of whom lost ground during the 1980s?
This period of policy reform is dated by Krueger as starting

with the Mexico debt crisis in 1982, and involved no less than a reappraisal of the appropriate role for government in promoting economic development. The consensus on the need for policy reform in many low income countries set the world stage for the stunning political and economic changes occurring in Eastern Europe and the Soviet Union today. These lectures integrate the broad sweep of historical patterns and the abstract economic rationale for policy change, with the detail of politically negotiated and frequently frustrated reforms that depend for their success on an elusive amalgam of bold local leadership and sustainable domestic alliances of personal interest groups. The lessons drawn from the era by Professor Krueger warrant the study of both students and scholars of economic development, political science, and international relations.

T. Paul Schultz
Director of the Economic Growth Center
Yale University, New Haven, Connecticut

Introduction

In the 1950s, one of the exciting fields in economics was economic development. Many newly independent countries were seeking rapid economic growth to "close the gap" between living standards in developed and developing countries. One legacy of the Great Depression was a strong distrust of markets; it was widely believed that market failures were pervasive, and largely accounted for underdevelopment, as it was then called.

Leaders of newly independent countries therefore believed that their responsibility included overseeing rapid economic development, with government as a leading sector. Many economists were challenged by the problems associated with governmental activities. Some focussed on developing input–output tables and planning models to improve decision making; some addressed questions of the "dual" economy in which a backward agriculture placed brakes on industrial development; and still others focussed on problems arising from "elasticity pessimism" surrounding the ability of developing countries to increase their export earnings.

Traditional economic theory focussed upon efficient allocation of resources, comparative advantage as a basis for trade, and other phenomena seemingly only distantly related to the central concerns of development economists, who believed that theirs was a "separate and different" branch of economics. Indeed, defenses of the government controls and import substitution policies normally were couched in terms of the "static" aspects of economic efficiency, and its inability to come to grips with "dynamic factors" in economic development.

Although some economists challenged the set of protectionist, interventionist policies adopted in the developing countries, their criticisms largely fell on deaf ears in the decades of the 1950s, 1960s, and 1970s, as the recorded rates of growth of developing countries far exceeded what had been regarded as feasible. After all, if real growth rates of 6, 7, and 8 percent were being achieved on a reasonably sustained basis, the overall policy stance could not be *that* bad!

It was only in the 1980s when it became evident that the observed growth rates had been achieved at the expense of costly foreign borrowing and accelerating inflation. Although there had been major successes with developmental efforts, as death rates fell and literacy rose, it was clear that growth rates achieved through the policies adopted in the earlier decades were unsustainable.

There was little question that bureaucratic controls, mounting public sector inefficiencies, and inward-looking economic policies accounted for much of the development crisis of the 1980s. To that extent, the inefficiencies of earlier policies were clear and the traditional economists' concerns with economic efficiency and incentives were seen to have been valid.

However, as country after country was confronted with falling real incomes and heavy debt-servicing obligations, another set of questions arose. That was, given the inappropriateness of the earlier policy stance, what was the best path to move from the status quo to policies more conducive to growth?

Interestingly, economic theory has little to say about the transition path from a highly controlled and regulated economic system to a system of market oriented incentives. Although one can call upon first principles – such as the credibility of announced policy changes, the need for appropriate incentives, and so on – the fact is that understanding of the reform process must come largely from analysis of empirical evidence of reform efforts.

During the 1980s, economists began to analyze these efforts based on the experience of individual reforming countries. Models were built, based upon stylized facts which helped understanding of various elements of the process. Questions were also addressed about the "timing and sequencing" of policy reforms.

In practice, leaders in country after country announced reform programs. In some instances, they were genuine; in other cases, however, they were at best half-hearted and inadequate. As announcements of "failed" reform efforts started to appear, critics began alleging that the process itself was at fault. Lack of understanding of the depth of initial difficulties, and the extent of needed reforms seemed to be a major factor contributing to these half-hearted efforts.

It therefore seemed appropriate, when invited to give the Kuznets Lectures, to focus on the need for reform, the reform process, and the determinants of the outcome. Much has been learned by experience with reforms in the 1980s. Doubtless, much more will be learned in the 1990s as the experience of recent reforms and of the Eastern European countries increases.

Simon Kuznets pioneered the understanding of development through his analysis of the quantitative aspects of the growth of nations. Systematic data on the economic policies of nations would perhaps permit a more focussed analysis of policy reform in developing countries. Nonetheless, careful analysis of empirical evidence is the primary basis on which understanding of policy reform in developing countries can be advanced.

I am heavily indebted to T. Paul Schultz for stimulating comments and encouragement, as well as for hospitality while visiting New Haven. Comments of many members of the Yale faculty at the time these lectures were presented were valuable in revising the text for publication. Arnold C. Harberger provided valuable comments upon the first two lectures in their penultimate form. David Orsmond provided capable research assistance. Nakil Choi ably prepared the index.

1

Lecture One
The Need for Policy Reform

In August, 1982, Mexico startled the world by announcing that she could no longer voluntarily service her debt obligations. The news was especially surprising because not only was Mexico an oil exporter whose terms of trade had improved sharply, but oil discoveries in Mexico had increased the volume of oil exports substantially. Soon after the Mexican announcement, many other developing countries were forced to announce that they, too, were unable to continue voluntary debt-servicing.

Initially, observers blamed the worldwide recession and high nominal interest rates for the "debt crisis", as it came to be called. It also became evident that the commercial banks, which had been large net lenders to developing countries since the first oil price increase in 1973, had sharply cut back their lending in the wake of the Mexican announcement. That greatly intensified the abruptness of the crisis and the severity of the impact on many developing countries.

As time passed, however, evidence mounted that the "debt crisis" had been in large part the result of deeper difficulties, which were then exacerbated by the events of the early 1980s. While those events accounted for much of the timing of the crisis, they by no means explained the severity. There were a number of countries for which the impact of worldwide conditions was as great, if not greater, as it was for the debt-impacted countries that were able continuously to service their debt *and* to achieve rates of economic growth at at least the rates they had achieved in the late 1970s.

Those countries – including most notably Korea and Taiwan – had at one stage economic policies similar to those in the heavily indebted countries.[1] However, they had undertaken major policy reform programs in earlier decades, and by the 1980s their economic structures and policies bore little resemblance to those of the countries whose economic growth had stalled and whose debt could not be voluntarily serviced.

As economic stagnation persisted in the heavily indebted countries, the international development community gradually came to recognize that the economic policies of the debt-crisis countries were radically different from those pursued by the more rapidly growing ones. From this recognition, it followed that a resumption of growth would not and could not take place, barring incredibly favorable unanticipated circumstances, without serious reform of economic policies. A few countries, such as Turkey and Chile, had begun the process of policy reform prior to the debt crisis, and continued to pursue them. Countries such as Mexico began reorienting their economic policies, and "Structural Adjustment Programs" became an important focus of support for World Bank and International Monetary Fund lending.

As the 1980s progressed, more and more countries' leaders announced or undertook "economic policy reform" programs. In some instances, these programs were very short-lived. In some other cases, they were followed with yet other "reform

1 In addition, there were some other countries, including notably India and Pakistan, which had policies similar to the heavily indebted countries but which had not borrowed extensively in the 1970s, accepting instead relatively slow rates of growth. Those countries were not subject to debt crises in the early 1980s, although efforts to alter economic policies to achieve more rapid growth of living standards were also made.

programs" within short periods of time. In a few cases, "reform" appeared to acquire a momentum of its own, and economic growth resumed.

By the late 1980s, when the necessity for policy reform was coming to be widely, if in some cases, grudgingly, accepted, the countries of Eastern Europe announced their intention to change economic policies. The dramatic nature of their changes, and the evidence regarding the poor economic performance that had preceded the reforms, focussed interest on the part of many in the policy reform process, and increased consensus on the necessity of reforms.

What was and still is necessary in many of the developing countries is a fundamental transformation of economic policies. Yet, in practice, *any* change in economic policies is described as a "policy reform program." Brazil underwent five "policy reform" programs in as many years without significant alteration in that country's fundamental economic problems.[2] Early in 1991, the Argentina government announced the eleventh "crash economic package" since President Carlos Menem had taken office in July 1989![3]

Unfortunately, the process of far-reaching policy reform, of the type needed in developing countries and Eastern Europe, is not well understood, and because of that many so-called programs have been "too little, too late," cosmetic, and otherwise destined to fail. Those apparent failures, in turn, have led some to question whether policy reform can work, and intensified political opposition to them. There has been confusion about the reasons why reform may be essential, what the alternatives to reform are, and what constitutes a reform program.

The purpose of these lectures is to provide an analysis of the

---

2 See *New York Times*, February 11, 1991, p. A9 for a description of the atmosphere at the time the fifth plan – another wage and price freeze – was announced. In Brazil, it was termed the "scud" plan, referring to the expected failure of the plan to hit its inflation target, while nonetheless causing random damage to the economy.
3 *Economist*, February 9, 1991, p. 44.

reform process, the reasons why it is essential, the difficulties it entails, and the payoff from successful reforms. Focus is primarily on policy reform in the developing countries, in part because the longer period of time during which reforms have been ongoing has provided empirical evidence to increase understanding of the process. An appendix contrasts the similarities and differences between the economic structures and situations of the developing countries undertaking reforms and of the Eastern European countries.

A necessary starting point is an assessment of the economic policies of those developing countries that encountered such great difficulties in the 1980s. The first part of this lecture provides an overview of broadly typical policies. The second part then examines the ways in which these policies were inimical to sustained economic growth, and indeed were unsustainable. A third part documents measures of government intervention and the economic performance for some developing countries and the fourth part draws conclusions.

1 The Economic Policies of a "Typical LDC"

Origins of Developing Countries' Economic Policies

Among the global changes that marked the end of the Second World War, one of the most important was the emergence of many former colonies as newly independent nations. During the late 1940s, the 1950s, and the 1960s, most of the previously colonialized areas attained independence. India, Pakistan, Sri Lanka, and Burma were among the first in 1947, with Indonesia following later in the decade. In the 1950s, the French left Southeast Asia and North Africa, and some of the sub-Saharan countries became independent. In the 1960s, most of the rest of the sub-Saharan African countries attained independence, and by the 1970s there were few colonies left.

At independence these former colonies shared an economic structure vastly different from that in most of the industrialized countries. In almost all of them, agriculture was the source of livelihood for more than half the population. Exports consisted largely of primary commodities, very often produced on estates or in mines that had been organized and managed largely by expatriates from the former colonial power. Manufacturing was a relatively small economic activity and typically consisted of small-scale enterprises producing simple consumer goods such as candles, matches, vegetable oil, textiles, apparel, and footwear.

Although living standards differed significantly among the newly independent countries, all were low by contrast with those in the rich countries. Moreover, indicators of the quality of life – educational attainment, life expectancy, nutritional status, infant mortality, availability of physicians and hospital beds, access to safe drinking water, and so on – were similar and reflected a picture of widespread poverty by contrast with the standards of the industrialized countries.

To be sure, some countries – including Turkey, most of Latin America, Thailand, and China – had earlier attained independence or never been colonies. But their economic structures were very similar to the formerly colonial countries, and there was a strong sense of affinity and shared experience among these poorer countries. Even when they had not been colonies, there was a widespread belief that the economic strength and well-being of the industrialized countries was somehow responsible for their lower living standards.[4]

---

4 Marxist doctrine, of course, asserted that the affluence of the developed countries had come at the cost of the developing countries. Similar doctrines arose from non-Marxist sources. Prebisch, for example, spoke of the "center" and the "periphery" and the ways in which asymmetries of the international economy transferred most of the gains in productivity to the "center" (Raul Prebisch, "Commercial Policy in the Underdeveloped Countries," *American Economic Review, Papers and Proceedings*, 49 (2), May 1959, pp. 251–73). W. Arthur Lewis' concept of a perfectly elastic labor supply could be interpreted to lead to the same conclusion (W. Arthur Lewis, "Economic Development with Unlimited Supplies of Labor,"

Nationalism was an important force in all of them. One of its important manifestations was the popular mandate, if not demand, very much shared by the modernizing elite, for rapidly rising living standards and a changing economic structure.

In part because poverty was so dominant in so many countries, and in part because of the political imperative for policies designed to accelerate economic development, all of these countries were regarded (and regarded themselves) as a group. Initially, they were referred to as "Third World" countries, or as "underdeveloped." Terminology later changed to "less developed countries," and finally to "developing countries." To a large degree, they have aligned together in international fora, such as the Group of 77 and in the United Nations Conference on Trade and Development. Multilateral institutions, such as the World Bank and the regional development banks, have oriented their activities to supporting the development efforts of governments in developing countries. Ideas and attitudes have also been widely shared, and scholars have focussed on such phenomena as "economic development," "politics of development," and the "sociology of development," treating the problems and experience of the Third World as being similar across countries with very different cultural and historic backgrounds, but different from the situation in industrialized countries.

The quest for modernization and for living standards similar to those in industrialized countries was therefore closely associated with nationalism. Observers noted the much larger share of industry in economic activity in developed countries: the presence of factories, and especially large-scale "heavy industries," was seen to be a critical difference between indus-

---

Manchester School 22 (2), May 1954, pp. 139–91). See Ronald Findlay for an elegant model of this result (Ronald Findlay, "Economic Development and the Theory of International Trade," *American Economic Review, Papers and Proceedings*, 69 (2), May 1979, pp. 186–90).

trialized and poor countries. In consequence, most countries'
politicians and policy makers sought to adopt policies that
would result in the "industrialization" of their countries.

Several interrelated strands of thought contributed to policy
formulation in pursuit of industrialization. First, there was
the widespread belief in the "weakness" of domestic economic
activities and their inability to compete with established
industries abroad. Second, there was a strong suspicion of the
market mechanism, and a belief that the government would
have to assume responsibility for development. Third, there
was a strong tendency to discount the value of traditional
economic activities.

The perception of "weakness" of domestic economic activities was especially great when observers noted discrepancies
in the size and structure of manufacturing activities. Whether
because of a belief that new industries in developing countries
could never compete unless protected, or whether policy makers believed in the "infant industry argument" that new industries generated dynamic externalities and required time to
become competitive, the authorities in all developing countries
adopted policies to foster "import-substitution." Since few
manufactures were produced domestically, it was assumed
that the "leading engine of growth" would be increases in
manufacturing production which would increase rapidly to
replace imports in domestic consumption. This was
implemented by taking measures to assure domestic producers
that once they began producing particular commodities, they
would be protected from foreign competition to the necessary
extent.

The second leg of policy – the suspicion of the market –
arose in part from the colonial experience, in part from the
tremendous impact of the Great Depression on the developing
countries, and in part from the intellectual atmosphere of the
times. It was generally believed that private producers were
too myopic, or too small, or too uninformed, to be willing
and able to undertake appropriate economic activities. Thus,
the government, it was thought, would need to do so. The
role of government was widely perceived to include not only

the infrastructure and social overhead activities which had been carried out by governments in industrialized countries during their development, but also the direct responsibility for economic activities traditionally regarded as being in the private sector, including agricultural marketing, establishment and operation of factories, and even the construction and management of hotels and other tourist services. In addition to this positive role, it was also thought there would have to be fairly tight regulation of private sector economic activity.

The third pillar – failure to attempt to build upon traditional strengths, especially in agriculture – of policy grew out of similar perceptions. On one hand, it was widely believed that the demands for primary commodities, the chief exports of almost all developing countries, were both price and income inelastic. As such, it was expected that world demand for these commodities would grow only slowly, and that therefore export earnings from those sources could not be counted upon to provide foreign exchange earnings.[5] On the other hand, peasants were generally viewed as "backward" and unresponsive to economic incentives. As such, there seemed to be no reason not to attempt to pull resources from agriculture for industrial development.[6]

5 It may be noted that this attitude contained the seeds of a self-fulfilling prophecy. Because policy makers believed that export earnings could not grow, they provided incentives that pulled resources away from traditional activities and into newly protected ones. It was an ironic consequence that supply shortfalls, rather than world demand inadequacy, brought about the very result that had been predicted.

6 This view was reinforced by casual inspection of the declining share of agriculture in developed countries. It was not initially recognized that agriculture's share in industrialized countries had declined *because* of rapid productivity growth. Cause and effect were essentially confused.

Similarities among Developing Countries' Policies

Starting as they did from evidently similar economic structures and aspirations and with common ideas as to the causes of economic "underdevelopment," the economic policies adopted by most developing countries in the 1950s and 1960s were remarkably similar in form and content. Nonetheless, there were differences in the extent to which policies were inimical to growth. Although Kenya and Ghana both discriminated against their agricultural producers, for example, it would appear that the degree of discrimination against agriculture in Kenya was less than half of that in Ghana.[7] Likewise, Turkey (prior to policy reforms which began in 1980) and Ghana both had significantly overvalued exchange rates for which they compensated with highly restrictive licensing systems over imports and controls over foreign exchange. In Ghana's case, however, the degree of overvaluation of the currency was so extreme that devaluation, when it came, increased the price of foreign exchange by 900 percent! Even that was not an exchange rate that could be expected to equalize the demand and supply for foreign exchange, and exchange controls were still used to contain excess demand. By contrast, the degree of overvaluation in Turkey was certainly far smaller.

For purposes of analyzing reform programs, I shall therefore start by setting up a straw man: the economic policies of a "typical" poorly performing developing country as of the late 1970s. These assertions will at first be documented with

7 Robert H. Bates, *Essays on the Political Economy of Rural Africa*, University of California Press (Berkeley), 1983. For an interesting essay focussing upon the contrasts between developing countries' policies, see J. Dirck Stryker and Hasan A. Tuluy, "Assistance to Ghana and the Ivory Coast," in Anne O. Krueger, Constantine Michalopoulos, and Vernon W. Ruttan (eds), *Aid and Development*, Johns Hopkins Press (Baltimore), 1989, chapter 15.

occasional statistics and illustrations. Thereafter, statistics capturing some aspects of economic policies for a group of developing countries are presented.

The Behavior of Governments

It is incredibly difficult for those in western democracies to appreciate or even comprehend the role of governments and of governmental economic policies in most developing countries. In part, this is because those in the industrialized countries are used to the inefficiencies and misallocations of their own governments' economic policies. They assume that others' governments have the same degree of inefficiency, ignoring three things. First, there is the fact that governmental inefficiencies in the industrialized economies were gradually introduced as they became rich. For developing countries, whose resources are very scarce, there is little margin for these excesses, and the growth cost of inappropriate economic policies can be extremely high. This is especially true because per capita income growth of 2–3 percent annually seems to suffice in most developed countries and requires real GNP growth of less than 3–4 percent. In most of the poorest developing countries, higher rates of population growth imply that real GNP growth must be 3 or more percent just to stand still, and 2–3 percent per capita income growth, which is still relatively slow if catch-up is to be achieved, would entail 5–6 percent growth in real GNP.

The second reason for a failure to appreciate just how poor economic policies can be is the comfortable western assumption that governments are responsive to their citizens, and are attempting to improve their welfare.[8] Although there

8 This assumption has in recent years been challenged, even for the industrialized countries. See, for example, James N. Buchanan, "Market Failure and Political Failure," *Cato Journal*, 8 (1), Spring/ Summer 1988, pp. 1–13. However, most observers would conclude that the extent to which policies detrimental to welfare can be adopted is far greater in many developing countries than it is in

are important differences among developing countries, there are many where officials and politicians appear little constrained in their behavior by the impact of their policies on the majority of their citizens. The third reason follows, in large part, from the second: economic policies in developing countries can be, and often are, far more inimical to productive use of resources than are the policies in the developed countries. Developed countries have, for example, tariffs, and occasionally quantitative restrictions on imports. These result in economic inefficiencies, and sometimes raise domestic prices of imported and import-competing commodities by as much as 50 percent. In many developing countries, tariffs and quotas are so extreme that domestic prices of double, quadruple, and even ten times the world price are not unheard of!

There are a number of countries, most of them in sub-Saharan Africa, where living standards have deteriorated at least over the past two decades.[9] In many of those countries, there is a suspicion that the lot of the "common man" has deteriorated even more than the average, as municipal services have deteriorated, if not disappeared, and as distribution networks serving farmers have broken down. Perhaps the saddest story I have heard from a developing country circulated at the World Bank in the mid 1980s: a World Bank team was surveying an area in Somalia by jeep for suitability for a particular agricultural project. The team stopped by the side of the road for a picnic lunch. Across the road, a very thin wizened old man was using a crude hoe to remove a few weeds, and the team members commented among themselves upon his low productivity. As they were packing up to resume

---

most developed countries. See Anne O. Krueger, "Government Failures in Development," *Journal of Economic Perspectives*, 4 (3), Summer 1990, pp. 9–23.

9 Sub-Saharan Africa is the most visible region of decline, but other countries, including Laos, Cambodia, Burma, and Argentina, are also estimated to have lower living standards now than two decades ago.

their work, the old man approached them. Addressing one of the team who spoke Somali, he politely requested permission to ask a question. When told that he could do so, his question was: "Please, sirs, can you tell me when independence will end?" The fact, of course, was that living standards were substantially lower than they had been under colonial rule. Presumably, the man's sons would have migrated to urban areas in search of employment, while low prices for agricultural commodities and the breakdown of the system for supplying inputs to agriculture and for distributing outputs contribute to agricultural misery.

In what follows, therefore, the policies of a "typical" developing country are described. While there is no actual country that precisely fits the policy profile described below, the extent of similarity in policy among them is remarkable. Of course, some developing countries had already changed policies in the 1960s and 1970s. The description provided here is intended to convey an idea of the types of policies that prevailed among those countries that had persisted with, or even intensified, the policies based upon the thinking of the 1950s.

Types of Policy Failures

Difficulties with economic policy have encompassed virtually every aspect of economic activity. In the "typical" developing country, the government has either assumed responsibility for operating, or has attempted to control, all large economic transactions. Even for the small traders and peasants outside the direct purview of government controls, the effects of other governmental policies have often been the major determinant of their livelihood.

Broadly speaking, one can think in terms of four types of economic policies. The first is those affecting macroeconomic stability, including especially inflation, but also the level of economic activity. The second is the provision of, or failure to provide, infrastructure services which are essential to private production. The third is direct undertakings by the public sector of economic activities where there are few of the characteristics traditionally associated with public services. The fourth is the set of controls and incentives used by governments that intentionally or otherwise affect the allocation of resources in the private sector.

There are obvious linkages between these policies. Direct economic undertakings by the government have often resulted in sizeable losses, thus contributing to the government's fiscal deficit and macroeconomic instability. Government controls over foreign exchange allocation, the fourth type of policy, have sometimes severely restricted the level of economic activity. Failure to provide infrastructure services severely impinges on the incentives confronting the private sector.

Moreover, there are both theoretical and empirical grounds for believing that the deleterious effects on economic growth of some of these policies increase over time. A fiscal deficit of x per cent of GNP, for example, will result in a lower rate of inflation in the first year it is experienced than in the tenth, as the real balances people are willing to hold begin to decline as they experience inflation.[10] Similarly, the first year of import licensing is likely to prove less inimical to efficient resource allocation than the tenth, both because existing inventories can provide flexibility and because the market behavior of the preceding year can provide a better guide to bureaucrats in their first-year allocations than in their tenth.[11]

The complications arising from interactions among policies and their cumulative effects are largely ignored here for ease of exposition. Each set of policies is discussed in turn. Thereafter, an effort is made to provide some systematic quantification to them for a small group of developing countries.

10 See Michael Bruno, "Econometrics and the Design of Economic Reform," *Econometrica*, 5 (2), March 1989, pp. 275–306.
11 To be sure, there are some phenomena that tend to mitigate the costs of given controls. As an import licensing system remains in operation, for example, smuggling and black markets may reduce the economic costs of the system.

Macroeconomic Policies   Many developing countries have experienced inflation at very high rates. The fifth Brazilian program undertaken within five years to control inflation was already mentioned. At the outset of that effort, the annual rate of inflation was in excess of 100 percent; by 1989, the rate of increase in consumer prices was 1,287 percent and in January 1991, prior to the fifth such effort, the *monthly* rate of inflation was 20 percent – an annualized rate of about 800 percent! Bolivia reached an annual rate of inflation of 40,000 percent prior to her stabilization effort in 1984; Chile reached 900 percent under Allende in the early 1970s; Ghana reached 120 percent in 1983; the Turkish inflation rate was over 100 percent in 1980; Uganda's rate exceeded 100 percent in each year from 1985 to 1988 and peaked at 238 percent in 1987.[12]

Inflation rates such as these in themselves cause enormous economic difficulties. But, in most developing countries, they are compounded by two things: efforts to control inflation through maintaining a nominal exchange rate or permitting its depreciation at a rate significantly below the rate of inflation; and maintenance of nominal interest rates at rates below the rate of inflation. Each of these, in turn, intensifies and exacerbates controls over private economic activity – through credit rationing and foreign exchange controls – discussed below.

These high inflation rates reflect large public sector deficits, which appear to have increased secularly. Developing countries as a group averaged central government deficits of just under 4 percent of GNP in the 1973–9 period, and of 5.5 percent in the 1980–7 period. In the 1980s, the *average* public sector deficit as a percentage of GNP for all western hemisphere developing countries was 4.19 in 1981, 6.73 in 1982, just under 6 in 1983 and 1984, 7.32 in 1985, and 8.94 in 1986.[13] For African developing countries, the average

12 Data from International Monetary Fund, *International Financial Statistics Yearbook*, 1990, p. 117.
13 Ibid., pp. 156–7.

reached 5.71 percent in 1986 and was 4.61 percent in 1987, the latest year for which data are available. Even these estimates, of course, understate the magnitude of the problem. On one hand, most governments confronting inflation practice varying degrees of "creative accounting," and a number of items are posted to the books only with a large delay, or are kept entirely off-budget.

An effort to diagnose the causes of the tendency for large and growing public sector deficits would require an in-depth study all of its own. Suffice it to say that, in many countries, economic inefficiencies of the sort described later in this section resulted both directly in larger public sector deficits (for example, as a result of greater deficits incurred by parastatal enterprises) and indirectly in tendencies for growth rates to slow down. Given the political imperative to deliver rising living standards, there was strong pressure on governments to increase their expenditures in an effort to maintain rates of economic growth. Simultaneously, economic policies often resulted in reduced abilities of governments to obtain revenue, either because economic activity moved into the "informal"[14]

14 The "informal" sector is the term used to describe those economic activities which are carried out, usually by individuals or small economic units, outside the purview of the laws and regulations of the government. Informal sector activities vary from country to country, but include: small-scale enterprises which pay less than the legislated minimum wage or avoid payroll taxes and other legislation surrounding employment; black and gray markets in which price controls, quality standards, and other regulations are not enforced; smuggling and other mechanisms which permit exporters to retain their foreign exchange and importers to import without obtaining their foreign exchange through official channels; and "curb markets" in which money lenders provide credit at interest rates higher than those permitted in the official market. For an analysis of informal labor markets, see Gary S. Fields, "Rural–Urban Migration, Urban Unemployment and Underemployment, and Job-Search Activity in LDCs," *Journal of Development Economics*, 2 (2), 1975, pp. 165–87. For an analysis of informal credit markets, see Ijaz Nabi, "Investment in Segmented Credit

sector or because governmental attention to the operation of parastatals and controls over private economic activity drained administrative resources that could otherwise have been used to enforce existing tax laws.[15]

An interesting question, and one that cannot be explored further here, is the extent to which inappropriate controls over the private sector and microeconomic policies contributed to, or possibly even caused, the tendency for growing public sector deficits. Certainly, there has been a strong tendency for large and growing public sector deficits to be associated with those countries whose economic policies provided inappropriate incentives for private sector activities.

Failure to Provide Infrastructure and Social Overhead Services   All analysts recognize the importance of infrastructure, as it has come to be called, and of education, health, and other services in the development process. Infrastructure is the term normally used to describe those facilities that are used in a wide variety of economic activities, including the roads, other transport (railroads, canals, ports) channels, communication facilities, power, and water. The human capital

---

Markets," *Quarterly Journal of Economics*, 104 (3), August 1989, pp. 453–62. For an account of the functioning of the informal sector in Peru, see Hernando de Soto, *The Other Path*, Harper and Row (New York), 1989.

15 Another factor in many developing countries was the growing power and political influence of the bureaucracy itself. This resulted in very high public sector wages relative to what might have been expected, which in turn contributed to distortions in the labor market in the private sector. It is estimated, for example, that the salaries of top civil servants, in proportion to per capita GNP, were 73 : 1 for Malawi, 82 : 1 in Kenya, 118 : 1 in Nigeria, and 130 : 1 in Uganda. This contrasts with ratios under 8 : 1 for the United States. For African data, see David B. Abernethy, "Bureaucratic Growth and Economic Stagnation in Sub-Saharan Africa," in Stephen K. Commins (ed.), *Africa's Development Challenges and the World Bank*, Westview Press (Boulder), 1988.

literature has, likewise, demonstrated the importance of investments in man (including especially education and health) in increasing people's productivity, and, therefore, incomes.

It has long since been recognized that provision of adequate infrastructure and social overhead services was a major responsibility of the state in many of the now-developed countries in the course of their economic growth. This responsibility was accepted by the political leaders in all developing countries. The First Indian Five Year Plan, for example, proclaimed that "an efficient and well-developed system of transport and communications is vital to the success of a plan of economic development."[16]

Yet, despite lip service, the "typical" developing country failed to provide infrastructure of a type that was conducive to facilitating increases in output and productivity. The hallmark of such a country is as much the government's neglect of infrastructure and social services as it is the emphasis upon controls over private economic activity and operation of parastatals in manufacturing and distribution activities.

For most infrastructure services, evidence as to neglect is anecdotal.[17] Unfortunately, there are few available data which document the quantity and quality of delivery of infrastructure and social overhead services. For a few, however, some data are available. One such infrastructure service is telephone communications. Table 1.1 provides estimates of the waiting length (in years) for a telephone in a number of developing countries in 1988. As can be seen, waits of more than five years were extremely common. Interestingly, in most of the countries listed where waiting times were relatively short (e.g. Malaysia), the overall policy stance has also been less inimical to growth. While there are obviously ways in

16 Government of India, Planning Commission, *Second Five Year Plan*, p. 459.
17 See, for example, the anecdotal evidence in de Soto, *The Other Path*.

Table 1.1. Number of Years' Wait for a Telephone in 1988

Country	No. of Years	Country	No. of Years
Algeria	8.5	Philippines	7.1
Argentina	21.9	Poland	12.2
Colombia	4.3	Sri Lanka	8.5
Egypt	27.1	Tanzania	10.9
Ghana	30.0	Thailand	3.6
Indonesia	7.8	Tunisia	5.0
Jamaica	22.3	Uruguay	2.8
Malaysia	0.6	Venezuela	8.1
Pakistan	10.0	Zimbabwe	5.3

Source: *World Bank News*, February 7, 1991, p. 2

which those needing phones manage to jump the queue, those ways are themselves sometimes costly. In India, for example, it is widely believed that side-payments to telephone operators permit the "switching" of lines to those making the payments. Thus, even those who have telephone service in theory are not always in practice able to use it. At any event, these numbers are indicative of the poor state of communication services in developing countries. As noted by the International Finance Corporation, "In many developing countries, even if you have a telephone, there is no guarantee that it will work. And if it does work, it is likely that you will have to dial the number several times before your call is connected."[18]

Port services are often similarly inadequate. Port congestion and delays in paperwork and customs procedures add significantly to demurrage charges.[19] In addition, however, they

18 *World Bank News*, February 7, 1991, p. 2.
19 After the 1973–4 oil price increase, the Government of Nigeria used some of its incremental revenue to increase its orders from foreign suppliers. Port congestion was so severe that over 200 ships were reported waiting for berth space to unload in mid-July 1975. See *Economist*, August 2, 1975, p. 70.

increase costs to domestic producers who are awaiting the arrival of spare parts, machinery, raw materials, and intermediate goods, and they can prevent exports that otherwise would be profitable.[20]

The poorly maintained state of roads is another frequently heard story. In some cases, roads have reverted to jungle for lack of maintenance. In others, potholes and other problems force trucks to travel at exceptionally low speeds, or to incur very high depreciation and maintenance charges.[21] It is estimated that the costs of operating vehicles on roads in such poor condition is 20–50 percent higher than it would be were roads adequately maintained.[22]

Electricity generation and distribution present similar problems. In Turkey in late 1979, electric power was in such short supply that the entire city of Istanbul was on a "rolling power outage" schedule, with power shut off for six hours at a time in different areas of the city. This naturally imposed sizeable costs on producers as well as consumers. In India, I once visited a factory, intended to produce rubber tires, in which the entire workforce had been engaged for the preceding three days in scraping rubber from tire moulds: the power had failed and, with power failure, the rubber had congealed in the moulds. The rubber was, of course, lost, in addition to the idle time for capital equipment and the necessary use of

20 See David Morawetz, *Why the Emperor's New Clothes are Not Made in Colombia*, Oxford University Press (Oxford), 1981 for an in-depth analysis of the difficulties Colombian exporters experienced in meeting delivery dates, and the ways in which that prevented their receipt of export orders.

21 The World Bank reported that, in 1988, there was a network of 1.8 million kilometers of main roads; one quarter of paved roads and a third of the unpaved roads outside metropolitan areas needed rebuilding at an estimated cost of $45 billion. This was 3–5 times greater than would have been the cost of maintaining the roads (and having use of their services). World Bank, *World Development Report*, 1988, p. 114.

22 World Bank, *World Development Report*, 1988, p. 114.

labor in restoring equipment to a useful state. In many instances, of course, firms protect themselves against power failures by installing backup generators. While these generators provide protection, to a degree, they are also much more costly than would be the necessary alterations to provide reliable electricity from a more central source.

Similar considerations pertain to railroads, postal services, irrigation facilities, and other infrastructure services provided by developing countries' public sectors. Large irrigation projects are built, but feeder channels to deliver water to individual fields are not; water is available to farmers only erratically; those at the end of the channel receive little water, while those near the source are overwatered. Lengthy delays in rail shipments, misrouted traffic, poor railbeds with consequent slow train speeds, and a shortage of railroad cars are all too frequent. Delayed and lost mail is such a frequent story that it is familiar to all who have attempted to communicate with colleagues or contacts in developing countries.

A number of factors contribute to these problems: the infrastructure facilities are typically underfunded, as politicians are reluctant to raise bus fares, electricity charges, telephone charges, and the like; politically, there seems to be more reward in funding the construction of a new facility than in maintaining an existing one; rapidly growing populations put pressure on existing facilities; administrative and organizational skills are scarce, and so on. Yet more fundamentally, the fact is that the attention of those in government in a "typical" developing country has been heavily focussed on the activities described below – operation of parastatal enterprises, and controlling private sector economic activity. The fact that interest and attention centered on these latter activities naturally meant that able politicians and bureaucrats gravitated toward them; only those unable to be promoted to managing steel mills or fertilizer factories were willing to accept the far less politically attractive jobs of scheduling rail freight, organizing postal deliveries, or clearing port congestion. Although the hypothesis that it was in large part the diversion of talent and attention that resulted in the pitiful state of infrastructure cannot be proven, there is casual evidence in support of the proposition. Korean infrastructure services in the 1950s were not reputed to be significantly different from those of the "typical" developing country, but Korean infrastructure services acquired a reputation for remarkable efficiency after policies were changed in the 1960s; Chilean management of ports and other public services is now taken as a model for much of Latin America, although in the 1950s and 1960s there was little to distinguish Chilean infrastructure services from those of other developing countries. Regardless of the reasons for it, the fact is that the "typical" developing country experienced government failure in the delivery of essential infrastructure in ways that lowered productivity and raised costs sharply for those who did attempt to produce goods and services.

Delivery of "social overhead" services, education and health, has not been quite as unsatisfactory as delivery of infrastructure. Literacy rates, and the ratios of those in the eligible range attending primary school, have risen markedly in most developing countries. Indeed, most indicators of the quality of life such as life expectancy, infant mortality, health care workers per thousand of population, have improved sharply.[23]

But even so, there has been a tendency to allocate a disproportionately large percentage of resources on high visibility activities, and far fewer on those less visible but with far higher rates of return. The World Bank, for example, estimates that the cost of saving an additional life through community health services or through preventive measures in developing countries is less than $200 and $500 respectively, yet less than 30 percent of total expenditures on health services in developing countries are spent on such activities. By contrast, the estimated cost of saving a life through curative measures is

23 Nancy Birdsall, "Pragmatism, Robin Hood, and Other Themes: Good Government and Social Well-Being in Developing Countries," World Bank, mimeo, May 1989, pp. 9–11.

$5,000 and yet 70–85 percent of public health care expenditures in developing countries are on curative measures.[24]

There is concern that the same sort of misallocation applies to education. Estimated social real rates of return to primary education in developing countries exceed 20 percent, while that to university education is estimated to be around 10 percent. Yet the subsidies to higher education are much greater than to primary education. This is not only a misallocation of public resources, but the implicit subsidies are going largely to the rich: the bottom 40 percent of the population in terms of income distribution is estimated to receive 2 to 17 percent of all public funds for higher education, which in turn are much greater than the amount allocated to primary education.[25] In Indonesia, it is estimated that the top 20 percent of the population in the income distribution receive 83 percent of funds publicly allocated for education, while the bottom 40 percent benefits from 7 percent.[26]

Moreover, governments have been unable to maintain basic infrastructure services, such as provision of safe drinking water and sewer collection, even in urban areas. Periods without running water, low pressure in the upper stories of buildings, and an absence of water lines to poorer areas of town are frequently encountered problems in a number of developing countries. There are also cases where sewage runs or seeps into the water supply with predictable consequences for the health of those who drink it. In some urban areas, even garbage collection has broken down. In the spring of 1990, a cholera outbreak was feared to be starting in Zambia, where garbage had been piling up for weeks without collection in urban areas, and where sewers had backed up.[27]

There is thus a substantial basis to believe that, even when

---

24 World Bank, *World Development Report, 1988*, p. 134.
25 World Bank, *Education in Sub-Saharan Africa: Policies for Adjustment, Revitalization, and Expansion*, (Washington, DC), 1988.
26 World Bank, *World Development Report*, 1988, p. 136.
27 *New York Times*, April 12, 1991, p. A8.

government expenditures are generating positive returns, a reallocation of expenditures even within those categories could vastly increase the real rate of return. Simultaneously, a shift of expenditures toward those activities (and away from some of those described below) would further enhance the effectiveness of public expenditures in developing countries.

As the data just presented for higher education indicate, there is another aspect of economic policy that deserves brief mention. That is, in most developing countries, subsidies and transfers absorb a sizeable proportion of government expenditures: in 1980, 39 percent of central government spending by low-income countries and 34 percent of spending by middle-income countries was allocated to subsidies and transfers.[28] These expenditures were usually promoted because of their supposed impact on the poorest in those societies. Yet, in practice, a disproportionate share goes to the upper decile or quartile of the income distribution. This was already mentioned for education, and data on health expenditures suggest the same thing. The upshot is that, whatever the rationale for subsidies and transfers, in the typical developing country they do not usually benefit the poor on net, and in many developing countries they actually worsen the income distribution.

State-Owned Enterprises The ideas and attitudes which resulted in a commitment to industrialization and a suspicion of markets also led to the view that the state should take a "leading role" in economic development, going far beyond the functions historically undertaken by states.[29] In consequence, "state-owned enterprises", sometimes referred to as public

28 World Bank, *World Development Report*, 1988, p. 117.
29 At that time, the prevailing opinion among economists was that there was little to distinguish between private and public ownership and management of economic activities. For a retrospective statement, see Jan Tinbergen, "Development Cooperation as a Learning Process," in Gerald M. Meier and Dudley Seers (eds), *Pioneers in Development*, Oxford University Press (Oxford), 1984.

sector enterprises, parastatals, or state economic enterprises – and here referred to as SOEs – were established in large numbers. In some cases, private activities – such as distribution of inputs for agriculture and purchases of farmers' crops – were taken over by the government. This was the case with many agricultural marketing boards.[30] In other instances SOEs were founded to produce commodities previously imported, or to undertake functions previously performed by private firms.

The proliferation of SOEs was enormous. Brazil had about 110 SOEs in 1960, and 485 in 1980; Mexico had 175 SOEs in 1960, and 520 in 1980; Tanzania had about 70 public sector enterprises in 1967 and 400 by 1981.[31] Not only did the number of SOEs grow, but their output grew even more rapidly, and the number of employees each enterprise had grew even more rapidly still. Their shares of investment and value added were substantial, amounting to as much as 80 percent and 40 percent in Zambia, and 70 and 20 percent in Burma.

SOEs were not confined to infrastructural activities – indeed, many of those functions were carried out directly by the central government. SOEs undertook mining operations, produced cigarettes, alcoholic beverages, textiles, clothing, machine tools, steel, and heavy electrical equipment, ran the hotels, operated banks, insurance companies, and shipping firms, held monopolies over the right to import and distribute goods deemed "essential," and ran wholesale and retail shops.

Parastatals were generally privileged in their access to cheap (overvalued) foreign exchange and imports, cheap credit (or zero cost Central Bank credits), electricity, available railroad or truck transport, telephone service, and other

30 See Anne O. Krueger, *A Synthesis of the Political Economy in Developing Countries*, Chapter 2. Volume 5 of Anne O. Krueger, Maurice Schiff, and Alberto Valdés (eds), *The Political Economy of Agricultural Pricing Policy*, World Bank, chapter 2. Johns Hopkins University Press (Baltimore), forthcoming.
31 World Bank, *World Development Report*, 1988, p. 76.

inputs. They were also usually exempt from import duties and other taxes. Despite that, their costs were high and mounting. In 1980, Baran Tuncer and I undertook a study in Turkey of total factor productivity growth. We obtained data on investment and other inputs by two-digit manufacturing sector, broken down into public and private components. We then computed levels and rates of growth of total factor productivity for public and private sector textile, chemical, electrical machinery, wood processing, and other two-digit industries in which SOEs and private firms both produced. To our amazement, we found that SOEs were invariably – regardless of sector – employing more than three times as much capital and about four times as much labor per unit of output as private firms, and we feared that no one would believe us.[32] Our astonishment increased as Turkish economists reacted to our numbers by asserting that we had vastly overstated the efficiency of Turkish State Economic Enterprises![33] It might be added that, by 1980, SOEs in Turkey incurred a deficit equal to more than 8 percent of GNP and were a major source of Turkish inflation, which at that time exceeded 100 percent annually.

SOEs absorbed a large share of investment and did not contribute as much to output. In India, for example, the public sector accounted for 62.1 percent of "total productive capital" and 26.7 percent of total employment in 1978–9. By contrast, it produced only 29.5 percent of value added in manufacturing. Private entities held only 32 percent of capital, but accounted for 68.2 percent of employment and 64.6 percent of value added in manufacturing.[34] And, while SOEs

32 Anne O. Krueger and Baran Tuncer, "Growth of Factor Productivity in Turkish Manufacturing Industry," *Journal of Development Economics*, 11 (3), December 1982, pp. 307–26.
33 Anne O. Krueger and Baran Tuncer, "Estimating Total Factor Productivity Growth in a Developing Country," World Bank Staff Working paper No. 422, October 1980.
34 See Pranab Bardhan, *The Political Economy of Development in India*, Basil Blackwell (Oxford), 1984, table 13, p. 102.

had absorbed about half of total investment, and therefore presumably should have been able to earn a sufficient return to finance additional investment, gross savings in the public sector never exceeded 4.4 percent of GNP up to 1981–2.[35]

I have already alluded to agricultural marketing boards (AMBs), which were usually given a monopoly over the distribution of inputs and outputs of agriculture, as private traders were typically outlawed. Although the stated reason for giving AMBs monopoly power was to stop the "exploitation" of farmers by private traders, in fact farmers often ended up worse off than before!

Given the large size of agriculture in developing countries, and the crucial role that increases in agricultural productivity can play in growth, the role of the AMBs was doubly deleterious to growth. Those boards were used as places in which to employ party members, politicians' relatives, and to hand out political patronage. Their expenses mounted sharply as a percentage of revenues, both because output pricing was often unrealistic[36] and because of falling productivity per worker. Stories are common of fertilizer being delivered after harvest, of collection points for agricultural commodities being so far away from the farm gate that producers could not deliver, of shortages of storage facilities so that part or all of the crop rotted, and of other breakdowns of the distribution system.[37]

35 Ibid., tables 10 and 11, pp. 97–9.
36 Panterritorial pricing was frequent. In some instances, the transport cost of the commodity to the nearest port exceeded the export price. See Doris Jansen, *The Political Economy of Agricultural Pricing Policy in Zambia*, World Bank Comparative Study Final Report, World Bank (Washington, DC), 1988.
37 For an example, see Nimal A. Fernando, "The Political Economy of Agricultural Pricing Policies in Sri Lanka since Independence," April 1987, mimeo, World Bank. In the Sri Lankan case, governmental inability to carry out policies was extremely harmful according to Fernando: the government was simply unable to send

To understand why this poor performance was virtually systemic, one has only to consider some of the challenges with which AMBs were confronted. A first and major one was to have in place an organization and physical facilities that could receive, grade, store, and trade in agricultural inputs and outputs. The challenge of this set of activities already taxes administrative capabilities and requires specialized knowledge of individual commodities. In most cases, however, civil servants or influential politicians were appointed to head them. Moreover, they were constrained by various politically imposed mandates: panterritorial pricing was one such mandate, selecting personnel (or hiring unwanted additional personnel) on criteria other than qualifications, paying prices unrelated to international or domestic market conditions, and so on. A typical challenge had to do with grading for quality: if inspectors were hired to assess the quality of the crop, and to compensate farmers differentially for different qualities of output (as is important with a number of crops), crop inspectors had three choices: they could grade honestly and accept very modest living standards, they could grade in response to the incentives (bribes) provided by the farmers, or alternatively they could grade most of the crop at lowest quality and pocket the difference. It should not be surprising that the second alternative was frequently adopted. One consequence was that export proceeds per unit fell systematically as quality diminished according to foreign examiners' evaluations, while domestic records indicate steady improvement in the quality of the harvest, as recorded by the inspectors! In Turkey, it is reported that the average scores on university entrance examinations were higher for a position in the college for

---

trucks to farm are as at harvest time to collect crops once it had given itself monopsony over farmers; storage facilities were inadequate to prevent deterioration of the harvest that was collected; and farmers were paid with long delays after collection of the harvest. There is also evidence that it was the larger and more affluent farmers, who were located nearer to major collection points, who benefitted most from Sri Lankan policies.

tobacco inspectors than for any other line of activity![38] The challenge presented by inappropriate pricing mandated by the government also had strong economic consequences. Consider the local manager of a marketing board charged with distributing cheap but scarce fertilizer (or credit, or pesticides) among local farmers. On one hand, there are hundreds of small units, of unknown size and little political influence. On the other hand, there are the large landowners, few in number, who are politically influential. Not surprisingly, in the typical developing country, the large wealthy influential landowners were the major beneficiaries of subsidized credit and inputs.

These sorts of difficulties applied not only to AMBs but also to parastatals quite generally: to those established in the manufacturing sector (of which there were many), as well as to those in transportation, communications, utilities, banking and insurance, and other activities. While analysis of the causes of these difficulties would go far beyond the scope of my topic today, the effects were highly deleterious for economic activity.

Most countries nationalized mines and other major revenue-earning activities, and gave many public sector enterprises monopoly power. One would thus anticipate that they were major sources of revenue for their governments. Instead, most required annual net transfers from their governments. In Sri Lanka, these transfers averaged more than 5 percent of GNP annually over the 1978–85 period; in Egypt, transfers averaged over 5 percent from 1978 to 1982, but fell to "only" 3.7 percent of GNP annually over the 1983–5 period.[39] As a consequence, the public sector enterprises were a negative factor for economic efficiency and growth both because of their own inefficient use of resources and because they placed pressure on government budgets. This pressure

38 Hasan Olgun, *The Political Economy of Agricultural Pricing in Turkey*, World Bank Comparative Study Final Report, World Bank (Washington, DC), 1990.
39 World Bank, *World Development Report*, 1988, p. 169.

then resulted either in a reduction in other governmental expenditures, such as the productive health and education expenditures already mentioned, or in accelerated inflation.[40] Indeed, efforts to reduce public sector enterprise deficits have often been essential elements of policy reform programs, and are discussed further in Lecture Two.

Controls over Private Activities   For the same reasons that governments in developing countries emphasized the growth of SOEs, they imposed a variety of controls on private economic activity. In many countries, these were all-pervasive. In India, for example, a firm could not operate at a level above its licensed capacity. It could not expand capacity without government permission, which was granted only after careful scrutiny of data submitted for cost–benefit analysis and after it was ascertained that capacity expansion licenses had not already been issued in sufficient volume to permit output to increase above planned levels. All imports were subject to license and, for capacity expansion, an import license could be applied for only after an investment license was obtained. In addition, the prices of many commodities were controlled. In some instances, commodities could not even be transported across state lines without government permission![41]

40 In principle, taxes could have been raised to cover the operating deficits of state owned enterprises. In practice, the "typical" developing country had raised taxes as much as was deemed feasible and had difficulty collecting those taxes already on the books. Although government expenditure and taxation decisions should, in principle, be made simultaneously, in the typical developing country it is reasonable to assume that the authorities decide on tax levels based on what they deem to be feasible, and additional expenditures are then covered by increasing the size of the public sector deficit or borrowing from abroad.

41 The above description approximately represents the control regime as it operated around 1970. See Anne O. Krueger, *The Costs and Benefits of Import Substitution: A Microeconomic Study*, University of Minnesota Press (Minneapolis), 1974, for an analysis of the system as it applied to the Indian automobile ancillary industry. See also

For the typical developing countries, controls over imports and exports and other foreign exchange transactions were by far the most important set of controls. However, regulations regarding the labor market and allocation of credit were also pervasive. Moreover, agricultural pricing policies imposed large costs on the agricultural sector. Each of these types of controls is briefly elaborated here. It should be noted, however, that the list covers only those controls that were prominent over a wide range of economic activities. Such a list fails to convey the extent to which government intervention in private economic activity was all-pervasive and detailed. In Brazil, for example, government efforts to encourage the development of a domestic computer industry went so far that it was illegal for a firm even to move a computer from one floor of its building to another without government permission![42]

Although controls over foreign trade may be regarded as the single most invasive and pervasive set of controls, the reason why they were so powerful in their impact was that control over imports gave government officials detailed control over every aspect of economic activity. Recall that the typical developing country adopted its development strategy from an initial position in which there was a very limited capability to produce manufactures, and in which most manufactured commodities were imported. As domestic firms sprang up to produce "import substitutes", capital goods were imported to build the factories, and very often imports of intermediate goods and raw materials were employed in the production process. Although the intention was to "save scarce foreign exchange", many of the import-substitution activities turned out to be "import intensive"![43]

Jagdish Bhagwati and T. N. Srinivasan, *Foreign Trade Regimes and Economic Development: India*, Columbia University Press (New York), 1975.

42 For a discussion of Brazilian computer regulation, see *Economist*, April 25, 1987, p. 26.

43 Carlos Diaz Alejandro, "On the Import-Intensity of Import Substitution," *Kyklos*, 18 (3), 1965, pp. 495–511.

The result was that firms were dependent on imported inputs for their ability to produce output. Tire producers needed rubber, carbon black, spare parts for machinery, and replacement moulds. Automobile assemblers could not produce without imports of engines, braking systems, and other commodities not produced in the domestic market. Even when engines came to be domestically produced (at high cost and low quality), imports of specialty steels, ball bearings, and other commodities were required.

In an environment in which import licenses were scarce and virtually determined the level of output of individual firms, government officials held the power of profit and loss over domestic import-substituting producers. Delays in obtaining licenses could cause partial or total shutdowns of sales, while receipt of a license guaranteed market share and profitability. In these circumstances, the ability of government officials to control economic activity was great, and an enterprise manager seeking profitability was better advised to allocate his energies to cultivating government officials and inducing them to view their applications favorably than he was to find lower-cost engineering solutions to assembly line problems. Entrepreneurs and managers spend their time "escorting their papers" through government offices and attempting to speed up approvals, because permissions for importation are subject to lengthy, erratic, and uncertain delays, with consequent build-ups of inventory, shut-downs of production, and other inefficiencies. It is not unusual to see spare machines sitting side by side with operational ones, the sole purpose being to enable the production to continue by enabling the "pirating" of the second machine while delivery of new parts is awaited. It is also not unusual to witness enterprising and resourceful mechanics reconciling metric and inch standards on equipment imported with different licenses, or finding means of getting a somewhat reasonable flow of materials through an assembly line despite the differing origins, dictates, and pieces of the machinery cobbled together from different foreign sources and made domestically to fill the gaps.

Because import-substitution policies pulled resources into high-cost import competing industries and discouraged exportable production, "foreign exchange shortages" usually emerged. When that happened, import licensing became even more restrictive, as the authorities were reluctant to reduce the importation of capital goods (which they believed essential for continued industrialization but which in fact substituted expensive capital for cheap labor) and hence maintained over-valued nominal exchange rates through restrictions on other imports, and prohibitions on imports of almost any goods that could conceivably be domestically produced.

In many instances, the authorities required that a firm seeking an import license prove that the commodity could not be domestically produced. In India, this took the form of requiring the license applicant to obtain letters from producers of products similar to the one he wanted to import that they could not meet his requirements. In the 1960s – a time of severe foreign exchange shortage – it was reported that an Indian exporter of tea was approached by the German importer, with the suggestion that it might be cheaper to put the tea in tea bags in India than in Germany. The exporter thereupon approached the government, seeking to import tea-bag paper with the appropriate porous qualities. Several months later, he was informed that he would have to obtain letters from all domestic producers of paper to the effect that they could not provide paper meeting his technical specifications. He proceeded to do so: all but one paper producer declared that he could not meet the specified standards. One producer, however, said that he could not produce white paper, but he could meet the standards with *brown* paper. The hopeful exporter took these certificates to the government. Four months later, he was informed that brown paper would be satisfactory, and that the Germans would have to learn to like it! Naturally, tea continued to be exported in bulk, and processed in Germany.

These sorts of procedures obviously discouraged exports. They also conferred a great deal of monopoly power on domestic import-substitution producers, whose consequent neglect (while they, too, were busy seeking their licenses) of quality control, costs, and delivery schedules became notorious.

Very high effective rates of protection – 1,000 percent was not infrequent – were a result. Because the structure of protection influenced the development of almost all industries, the consequences were an increasingly large share of new resources and GNP being allocated to ever-higher cost activities, with a consequent inevitable retardation of growth.[44]

Inefficiencies were even greater, however, because of the structure of developing countries and interactions with other policies. Protection of some economic activities, i.e., import-substituting industries, is necessarily discrimination against others. In this case it was potential exportable industries and agricultural exportables which bore the brunt of the discrimination.[45] But because of the belief that investment had to be accelerated to accomplish rapid growth, developing countries have generally experienced more rapid inflation from deficit-financing than have the major OECD countries. They were, however, reluctant to adjust their nominal exchange rates. Policy makers have preferred to restrict (again, usually through licensing) imports to available foreign exchange earnings on the theory that that would make invest-

44 For a fuller analysis of the ways in which the trade and payments regime resulted in decelerating growth, see Anne O. Krueger, "Comparative Advantage and Development Policy Twenty Years Later," in Moshe Syrquin, Lance Taylor, and Larry E. Westphal (eds), *Economic Structure and Performance*, Academic Press (Orlando, FL), 1984.

45 See Anne O. Krueger, Maurice Schiff, and Alberto Valdés, "Agricultural Incentives in Developing Countries: Measuring the Effect of Sectoral and Economywide Policies," in *World Bank Economic Review*, 2 (3), September 1988, pp. 255–72. The impact on farm real incomes of the higher prices farmers had to pay for intermediate and consumer goods appears to have been as large as the impact of overvalued exchange rates and suppressed producer prices in many instances.

ment goods cheap and thus increase the rate of investment. Predictably enough, this interaction between the inflation and the trade regime has resulted in the disappearance of all but those traditional primary commodities where rents to a scarce factor (land or mineral resources) permitted production to continue, at least covering the marginal cost of labor and capital.[46]

Reducing the real price of foreign exchange has interacted with agricultural pricing policies in costly ways. A major consequence of exchange rate overvaluation was that exports of traditional agricultural commodities diminished, or at least failed to grow, while no new agricultural export commodities emerged. Recent estimates from the World Bank Comparative Study of The Political Economy of Agricultural Pricing Policies in Developing Countries suggest that agricultural producers' real incomes were reduced three ways: (1) the overvaluation of the exchange rate reduced the real returns to agricultural exports relative to home goods; (2) the protection accorded to import-competing goods raised the relative price of the manufactured commodities that farmers would consume and thus lowered the purchasing power of their earnings; and (3) other governmental interventions – including notably AMBs – raised the margin between border price of exports and farmgate price, thus further lowering returns to farmers. In Ghana, for example, the real price received by cocoa farmers for their beans by the early 1980s was less than 10 percent of what it had been in the 1950s, although the world price at that time was about the same. The predictable consequence was that Ghana lost her preeminent position as a cocoa exporter; her exports fell in volume terms by 71 percent from the mid 1960s to 1984, as domestic production

46 One of the arguments often heard about a developing country is that it is "entirely dependent" on the international prices of one or two primary export commodities. This dependence is normally viewed as "structural." In fact, it is often the outcome of a process in which all profitability of exporting has been removed except in those few instances where some resource rent remains.

fell by two-thirds from 1960 to the early 1980s.[47] But Ghana was not alone; Sudanese exports of cotton fell off dramatically in response to similar shifts in incentives; Argentine exports of beef and wheat fell as domestic consumption rose in response to low domestic prices and production stagnated or fell; Nigerian production of exportable crops diminished sharply and exports consequently fell; and so on.

While exchange rate policy, cost-raising aspects of import substitution, and AMBs lowered the prices received by farmers for export crops, many governments subsidized domestic consumption of staple food commodities. In these instances, either they suppressed the producer prices (in order to avoid the budgetary impact of these policies) or they incurred sizeable budgetary deficits on that account. In Egypt, food subsidies became so large that farmers bought subsidized bread to feed their poultry because it was cheaper than animal feed,[48] and in some years the budgetary cost of subsidies on wheat alone exceeded 10 per cent of government expenditures, with a high of more than 18 percent in 1974.[49]

The virtually universal discrimination against agriculture among developing countries resulted in a decline in their share of world agricultural exports from 32 percent in 1950 to 16.5 percent by 1975.

47 See J. Dirck Stryker, *The Political Economy of Agricultural Pricing Policies: Ghana*, World Bank Comparative Study, Final Report, World Bank (Washington, DC), 1988.

48 Jean-Jacques Dethier, *The Political Economy of Agricultural Pricing Policy in Egypt*, World Bank Comparative Study Final Report, World Bank (Washington, DC), 1988.

49 For other examples, see for example Ammar Siamwalla and Suthad Setboonsarg, *The Political Economy of Agricultural Pricing Policies: Thailand*, World Bank Comparative Study, Final Report (Washington, DC), 1988. In Thailand, the urban rich appear to have been the largest gainers from subsidies. See also Grant Scobie, "Food Subsidies in Egypt: Their Impact on Foreign Exchange and Trade," International Food Policy Research Institute Report No. 40 (Washington, DC), August 1983.

In addition to agricultural pricing policies, governments often imposed price controls over other commodities. Controls are frequently encountered on prices of foods, pharmaceuticals, bus and other passenger transport (often including automobiles), newspapers, and a variety of other items deemed "essential" to either consumers or producers. These controls are a continuing feature of the landscape, and are separate from the overall price controls frequently imposed as part of anti-inflation programs.

If regulations and licensing are pervasive in commodity markets, they are equally encountered in factor markets. In many countries, minimum wage rates are set at levels well above realistic levels, and requirements for training workers, for provision of housing and fringe benefits, and for social insurance taxes raise labor costs well above levels consistent with full employment of labor, given levels of labor productivity. In addition, employers are often prohibited from firing workers who have been employed for longer than a specified time period – often one, two, or three years. The negative incentives for employing labor that these regulations provide has, naturally, led producers to choose relatively capital-using production techniques in countries where the theory initially was that capital was the *scarce* factor of production! In most instances, of course, regulations governing employment can be enforced only over large-scale enterprises – typically the new, import-substitution firms. The consequence has been the emergence of an "informal sector", in which the labor market clears at wages way below those prevailing in the "modern sector," but in which jobs in the latter are greatly sought after because of high rates of pay, fringe benefits, and economic security that they confer. One consequence is often open unemployment, of the type described by Harris and Todaro.[50] Another consequence is

50 John R. Harris and Michael P. Todaro, "Migration, Unemployment and Development: A Two Sector Analysis," *American Economic Review*, 50 (1), March 1970, pp. 126–42.

that exports, which would presumably be developed based in part on comparative advantage in labor-using activities, are discouraged since it is difficult, if not impossible, for exports to assume sizeable proportions outside of the formal sector of an economy.[51]

Whereas regulation of the labor market is a frequent phenomenon in "typical" developing countries, credit controls are virtually universal. Ceilings on nominal interest rates the banks may charge are normally set well below the rate of inflation. Banks are then normally instructed as to what percentage of, or how much, credit should be allocated to various economic activities, either by sector or by firm. In many instances, interest rates are also set differentially for different economic activities.[52]

For firms fortunate enough to be allocated credit, the subsidy element can be substantial. For those without access to the formal credit market, the cost of informal credit can be much higher. The net result is yet an additional incentive for import-substitution firms (which normally are among those favored with access to preferential credit) to employ capital-using techniques and to raise the costs of using capital in the informal sector.[53]

51 See, for example, the data presented in Anne O. Krueger, *Trade and Employment in Developing Countries, Synthesis,* University of Chicago Press (Chicago), 1983, chapter 7.

52 See Maxwell Fry, *Money, Interest and Banking in Economic Development,* Johns Hopkins University Press (Baltimore), 1988.

53 A number of economists have insisted that "financial repression," through credit rationing and controls over the banking system, has been the single most important source of economic inefficiency in developing countries. Foremost among the proponents of this view has been Ronald I. McKinnon. See his *Money and Capital in Economic Development,* Brookings Institution (Washington), 1973.

2 The Effects of These Policies on Economic Growth

Factor Accumulation and Efficiency

In early thinking about economic development, a starting point for analysis was the proposition that developing countries were trapped in a vicious circle: they had low per capita incomes because they had little physical capital per worker with which to work; and their savings rates were low because they had low per capita incomes.

With the benefit of the lessons that have been learned about development, the above statement might be amended in two ways: first, the low stock of human capital should be added to the list of causes of low per capita incomes; and secondly, it would be recognized that higher savings rates by themselves are not a guarantee of higher growth rates, in large part because of the effects of the sorts of economic policies described above.

For present purposes, however, the point I wish to make is a different one: although everyone would still agree that savings rates of 6–8 percent of GNP, such as were observed in South Asia in the 1940s and 1950s, were not adequate to permit reasonable rates of growth, it is now widely recognized that increasing savings rates alone is no guarantee that growth will accelerate. When economic policies are conducive to increasing inefficiencies and falling real rates of return on investment over time, increases in the savings rate will be essential simply to prevent a decline in the overall rate of economic growth.

There was a sizeable potential for development that arose from the initial development policies and plans: rising savings rates could permit investment in a variety of activities, including education, health, transport, communications, and utilities, that were highly productive. These investments in themselves provided ample scope for increased rates of growth of real GNP in the 1950s and 1960s. Simultaneously, starting from positions in which the public sector was extremely small and most activity was agricultural, the initial costs of resource misallocation were small, and offset in large degree by the rising savings rate and the large returns that could be reaped by investment projects that did yield high rates of return.

Even when investment was allocated to manufacturing and other activities that required governmental subsidies and/or heavy protection against imports, the first industries so favored were often those which used labor-intensive processes and were not too uneconomic. However, once textiles, footwear, some food processing, and other light labor-intensive activities had begun, additional investments could not increase capacity more rapidly than the rate of growth of demand, and new investments were directed toward industries with far greater cost disadvantages relative to developed countries. In part, this was because they were capital-intensive and, in part, this was because the scale on which it was expected they would operate was very small. These industries were not developed with any intent to take advantage of the export market: the sorts of incentives that were used to encourage import substitution did not affect exports.

Hence, growth could initially be fairly rapid as politicians turned their attention to attempting to achieve economic growth. Two exogenous factors increased this possibility: first, foreign aid from individual donor governments, and foreign capital flows from the international institutions, permitted an even greater increase in investment rates than the rise in domestic savings rates. The overall level of foreign aid permitted an excess of 2–3 percent of GNP of investment over savings, which was a considerable amount against the backdrop of one-digit savings rates. In some countries, of course, the contribution of foreign aid was significantly larger.

The second exogenous factor was the buoyancy of the international economy: the international economy as a whole grew extremely rapidly in the 1950–75 period. Even for countries whose policies were inimical to the expansion of their exports, the buoyancy of the international economy permitted their export shares to decline less rapidly than they otherwise would have. Thus, India's exports, which were 1.9 percent of total world exports in 1950, fell to 0.6 percent of world exports by 1972, although they grew in dollar value from $1.1 billion to $2.4 billion. A seldom-noted fact of the quarter-century after 1948 is that, with world trade expanding at an unprecedented rate, the share of the developing countries in that trade fell drastically: from 38 percent in 1950 to 29 percent in 1960 to 24 percent in 1970.[54]

Sustainable and Unsustainable Growth

Over time, however, the size of the public sector rose, controls intensified, and the resource misallocation costs of policies mushroomed. The size of the public sector increased for a variety of reasons. As was already seen, the government was regarded as the "leading sector" for growth so a very high fraction of new investment resources was funneled toward public sector activities and SOEs, and new SOEs were established to take on new functions. Simultaneously, existing SOEs expanded their staffs, both because they wanted to expand their activities and because political pressures for increased employment mounted. The costs of subsidy and transfer programs rose, and political pressures also resulted in increased expenditures. Although the authorities imposed high marginal tax rates in many cases, in most developing countries, as seen above, a tendency toward larger fiscal deficits also resulted.

Controls also intensified for a number of reasons. First, people began to find ways to evade controls, and as those evasions were discovered, new rules and mechanisms were put in place in an effort to prevent them. In Turkey in the 1950s, for example, newspapers, magazines and books were freely importable while most other commodities were subject to fairly stringent import licensing. It was finally noted that Turkish imports of the London *Times* were far in excess of

54 Data are from *International Financial Statistics Yearbook*, 1990, World Exports Table.

what one might have predicted on the basis of demographic and income characteristics. Upon investigation, it turned out that the Turkish paper used to make cigarettes was vastly inferior to foreign-made cigarette paper. However, imports were not permitted, and enterprising Turks discovered that the paper in the London *Times* made far better cigarettes than did domestic paper! The regulations governing imports of books, magazines and newspapers were subsequently tightened. In India, tractor parts produced domestically were not eligible for importation, and small tractors could not be imported because they could be domestically produced. Large tractors, however, were importable and, to everyone's consternation, demand for large tractors shot up sharply. Investigation showed that these tractors could be imported, and their parts used in the production of small tractors, at lower cost (and higher quality) than the available domestic parts! Import licensing regulations were, once again, tightened. In these, and other, instances, additional procedures and regulations designed to deter evasion also resulted in increased delays and a larger bureaucracy needed to administer regulations.

The resource misallocation costs of the same controls and regulations also increased. As has been well documented, as the "easy" import-substitution opportunities were used up, the costs of additional investments in new import-substitution activities rose. Even Raul Prebisch, one of the original architects of the import-substitution strategy, by the early 1960s concluded that import-substitution would not serve as a long-term vehicle for growth.[55] Incremental capital–output ratios rose, as more capital-using investments further from labor-abundant developing countries' comparative advantages were undertaken. Simultaneously, as the structure of industrial production became increasingly complex, the resource misallocation costs of bureaucratic controls increased. As the num-

55 Raul Prebisch, "Towards a New Trade Policy for Development," UNCTAD Conference E/Conf. AG13, United Nations, 1964.

ber of intermediate goods and spare parts required to sustain production increased, the costs of bureaucratic delays, of being required to use inappropriate domestically produced goods, and of domestic monopolies increased.

Simultaneously, export earnings grew more slowly than GNP, both because new resources were increasingly allocated to "import-substitution" and domestic activities and because overvalued exchange rates directly discouraged them, as discussed already. Also, corruption grew and lobbying activities increased, as more and more individuals recognized the opportunities for gain that obtaining concessions from the government entailed. In some countries, it is judged that the longer-term costs of corruption may exceed those of the resource misallocation resulting from developmental policies of the sort I described.[56]

Inevitably, rates of growth began to fall. In some instances, the deceleration was rapid, and a balance-of-payments crisis led to immediate adjustments in policy. Whether these adjustments were mere "tidying up" operations to permit a resumption of the old policies, or whether they were fundamental changes, varied from country to country.[57] When changes were fundamental, as in Korea in the early 1960s, the growth rate could accelerate sharply, with spectacular consequences for the entire body politic.

For other countries, the retardation in the growth rate came more slowly. In some instances, this was because policies were not quite so antithetical to the efficient allocation of new and existing resources. In other instances, favorable terms of trade developments permitted a continuation of policies that

56 I. G. Patel, "On Taking India into the Twenty-First Century," *Modern Asian Studies*, 21 (2), pp. 209–31.

57 See Anne O. Krueger, "The Importance of Economic Policy: Turkey and Korea," in Henryk Kierzkowski (ed.), *Protection and Competition in International Trade*, Basil Blackwell (Oxford), 1987, for a sketch of the difference in policies that can arise depending on whether changes are intended to permit a continuation of the system or to change it.

might otherwise have resulted in balance of payments crises. It is arguable that the Philippines might fall into this category; certainly, Mexico was able to delay her crisis until 1982 because of the rapid increase in oil export earnings.

For present purposes, however, the point is somewhat different. That is, given the inconsistency of the economic policies adopted with the objective of attaining a reasonable rate of economic growth, sustained economic growth is not possible. In the short run, there are several things the authorities can do: (1) they can increase public expenditures and total investment; (2) they can borrow more from abroad; or (3) they can accept a falling rate of economic growth. The first two of these alternatives are a short-run solution and consistent, over that time period, with maintaining economic growth. The third, of course, is to accept a declining rate of economic growth.

None of the three alternatives provides a permanent resolution of the policy inconsistency, but each one buys time for politicians, and permits avoidance of issues arising out of the policy inconsistency. In the first case, lip service may continue to be given to the goal of more rapidly rising living standards and rapid economic growth; in practice, however, that objective is subordinated, at least over the short and medium run, to other political considerations. Countries such as Ghana, Sudan, Tanzania, and Zambia in Africa appear to have followed this path, as have Burma and Argentina, to name some of the more extreme and visible examples.

The second alternative – offsetting the diminishing returns to incremental resource accumulation by increasing the rate of resource accumulation – is again not sustainable indefinitely. But a large number of countries increased their savings rates, and maintained apparently reasonable rates of growth, by increasing the rate of investment, while consumption grew much more slowly. The Peoples' Republic of China provides a case par excellence of this mode: the savings rate apparently reached well over 30 percent prior to the reforms of the late 1970s; the evidence suggests that living standards were no higher than they had been two decades earlier, although real GNP had increased enough to provide for the increased investment rate and also to offset population growth. In Costa Rica, to provide another example, investment as a percentage of GNP rose from 17 to 29 percent from 1960 to 1981, and government expenditures rose from 10 to 18 percent of GNP; private consumption fell from 77 to 60 percent of GNP over the same period. Thus, if one examines the path of real GNP, the rate of growth appears to have been about a fairly respectable 5.9 percent annually. If, however, one calculates the growth rate of real private consumption, it was just under 4 percent annually, resulting in a growth rate of per capita consumption of 1.3 per cent. During the 1980s, for reasons that will be discussed below, Costa Rica and many other countries which had used this path to reconcile inconsistent policies experienced sharply reduced growth, if not declining output.

The third alternative – reliance upon foreign resources (and, occasionally, good fortune) to compensate for diminishing returns to unsustainable policies – was adopted by many countries, especially in the 1970s after the first oil price increase. Perhaps the most dramatic recent instance of unsustainable growth was Peru in the mid-1980s. Alan Garcia became President of Peru in 1985 on a populist platform. He immediately increased government spending, while simultaneously imposing controls on prices. In the short run, there was a sizeable increase in domestic real incomes, although it was accompanied by a burgeoning current account deficit and a failure to service debt. Within two years, of course, the Peruvian economy was virtually in free-fall, as Peru had exhausted international reserves and could no longer obtain even suppliers' credits.[58]

The stellar examples of countries maintaining growth over a longer time period with unsustainable policies are Egypt

58 Rudiger Dornbusch, "Macroeconomic Populism," *Journal of Development Economics*, 32 (2), April 1990, pp. 247–77.

and Mexico. In the former case, Egypt received massive foreign aid and, in addition, experienced sharply increased export earnings from oil. In the latter case Mexico augmented rapidly rising export earnings with foreign capital inflows at a rate so rapid that the debt–service ratio did not even fall during the 1970s. There were huge oil discoveries in Mexico, and two sharp increases in their real price of oil in the period from 1973 to 1982. Despite that, Mexico's current account balance deteriorated over the period, as Mexican expenditures outpaced income even during those buoyant times.

Among the countries relying on any of these three alternatives, there were nonetheless occasional difficulties. As already mentioned, balance of payments crises often led to some adjustments as policy makers decided to approach the International Monetary Fund when economic dislocation became sufficiently severe. These adjustments, however, were often taken more to provide short-term correctives to imbalances than to change the fundamental incentives and policies that guided resource allocation and growth.

In Turkey, for example, a classic balance-of-payments crisis occurred as early as 1958. By the time that Adnan Menderes, then Prime Minister, was willing to approach the international community for assistance, production had dropped sharply as an inability to finance imports of petroleum products in a country with no domestic oil had brought the transportation system virtually to a halt. The choice that was faced in the summer of 1958 was to be unable to transport the harvest to port or market, or to make alterations in macroeconomic policy. These alterations were made reluctantly, but there was a massive devaluation (from LT2.8 per dollar to LT9 per dollar), and government expenditures were subject to ceilings in a manner which sharply reduced the fiscal deficit. The consequence was a rapid decline in the rate of inflation – from 25 percent to virtually zero within the space of 12 months – and a resumption of moderate economic growth, averaging around 7 percent annually over the period from 1959 to 1968. The fundamental trade and payments regime was unaltered, however, so that by the late 1960s, and again in the late 1970s, balance-of-payments difficulties had reemerged and another devaluation was undertaken.

3 The Record

It is difficult to capture statistically the extent to which policies were inimical to reasonable allocative efficiency and growth. However, in an effort to provide some nonanecdotal evidence to substantiate the case that policies were chaotic, the data in tables 1.2 and 1.3 were assembled.

The top panel of table 1.2 provides data on variables that are broadly correlated with some of the policies discussed in section 1; the lower panel records data on economic performance for the same countries. Data are presented for ten countries: Bolivia, Botswana, Brazil, Colombia, Ghana, Korea, Mauritius, Thailand, Turkey, and Zambia.

Five variables were found to serve as indicators of the reasonableness of economic policies. The first is the real interest rate, taken as the average deposit rate deflated by the rate of inflation, both as reported in *International Financial Statistics*. The second column gives the fiscal surplus (if a positive number) or deficit as a percentage of GDP. Column 3 provides an estimate of the rate of growth of real government expenditures, and column 4 gives an estimate of the ratio of government capital expenditures to total government expenditure. To attempt to reflect the extent to which the trade and payments regime was distorted, the black market premium, expressed as a percentage of the official nominal exchange rate, is reported.

For each country, these data are reported separately for four time periods: 1961–70, 1971–6, 1977–82, and 1983–8. Any subdivision of time is arbitrary, of course, especially since policies were changed on different dates in different countries (see table 1.3). The last five columns of table 1.2 gives indicators of economic performance during the comparable time periods. These include the level of real per capita GDP at the end of the period (column 6), the rate of growth of real GDP per capita (column 7), the rate of inflation as reflected in the consumer price index (column 8), the ratio of investment to GDP (column 9), the rate of growth of exports of goods and services (column 10), and the current account surplus (column 11) and the savings ratio (column 12), both expressed as a percentage of nominal GDP.

In Ghana, for example, the 1977–82 period witnessed a real interest rate which was, on average, a negative 33 percent, with a fiscal deficit equal on average to 8.4 percent of GDP. By this time, government could no longer continue to offset poor economic performance by increasing resource accumulation: the real growth of government expenditures was a negative 13 percent. This set of policies resulted in an average rate of *decline* of real per capita income of 3.6 percent annually, and an average rate of inflation of 68 percent. The ratio of total investment to GNP fell to 6 percent, and exports grew at only an average annual rate of 1 percent. All of this happened despite the fact that the current account was in deficit, as the savings rate fell to about 6 percent of GDP.

By contrast, Korea in 1983–8 had a positive real interest rate of 5.8 percent, the government budget was in deficit about 0.2 percent of GNP, the real growth rate of government expenditures was about 6 percent (which was about equal to the rate of growth of income and maintained the government share approximately constant), and there was virtually no black market premium. Korea's real GDP per capita during that period grew at an average annual rate of 8.8 percent, inflation averaged a moderate 3.5 percent, total investment stood at 29 percent of GDP, and export earnings grew at an average annual rate of 16.3 percent. The Korean current account surplus averaged 2.6 percent of GDP as the saving ratio reached 33.2 percent, and Korea was able to reduce her outstanding foreign debt substantially during the period.

Several phenomena may be noted. First, there is the tendency for the growth performance of countries with unrealistic

Table 1.2. Measures of Relative Economic Performance, 1960 to 1988[a]

	Measures of Government Intervention					Measures of Economic Performance						
	Real Interest Rate[b] (%)	Fiscal Surplus to GDP[c]	Real Growth Govt Exp.[d] (%)	Gov't Capital Exp.[e]	Exchange Premium (%)[f]	Real GDP per capita[g]	Growth GDP per capita[h]	Inflation (CPI)[i] (%)	Invest. Ratio to GDP[j]	Export Growth[k] (%)	Current Account Surplus[l]	Savings Rate to GDP[m]
Bolivia: 1960 = $882												
1961–70	10.1	n.a.	n.a.	n.a.	13.4	1237	3.4	5.5	14.7	9.4	n.a.	22.0
1971–6	–3.4	–1.8	n.a.	2.7	21.9	1530	3.6	17.8	20.0	21.8	0.2	27.4
1977–82	–10.1	–7.1	14.2	10.2	25.8	1294	–2.8	35.9	17.7	8.1	–5.2	20.1
1983–8	–80.2	–11.5	–4.0	6.0	62.1	1017	–3.9	558.1	10.4	–6.4	–5.9	10.3
Botswana: 1960 = $493												
1961–70	n.a.	n.a.	n.a.	n.a.	7.7	881	6.0	20.5	20.5	8.7	n.a.	–5.7
1971–6	n.a.	–4.3	22.6	34.8	16.2	1093	3.7	18.3	48.5	31.9	0.5	23.9
1977–82	–1.8	–0.7	13.8	28.7	n.a.	1555	6.1	12.5	39.4	18.8	–7.6	18.0
1983–8	0.3	15.6	13.8	18.4	26.9	2070	4.9	9.2	25.5	19.6	16.1	26.8
Brazil: 1960 = $991												
1961–70	n.a.	n.a.	n.a.	n.a.	12.8	1782	6.0	43.5	22.9	7.0	n.a.	20.3
1971–6	n.a.	0.2	8.1	6.0	17.8	2805	7.9	24.3	26.8	24.3	–5.0	20.7
1977–82	16.1	–1.8	14.0	6.4	25.2	3191	2.2	68.2	21.6	13.7	–4.3	20.8
1983–8	18.3	–9.0	15.3	4.1	52.6	3434	1.2	237.8	15.9	6.1	–1.5	19.3

Colombia: 1960 = $1344

1961–70	−2.6	n.a.	n.a.	n.a.	21.3	1711	2.4	11.0	19.2	4.0	n.a.	18.1
1971–6	−2.2	−0.7	2.5	n.a.	11.0	2191	4.2	18.3	16.5	16.4	−0.9	18.7
1977–82	1.3	−1.5	11.1	28.8	1.5	2573	2.7	25.6	19.3	8.5	−1.5	19.4
1983–88	5.5	−2.8	0.7	20.7	75.4	2846	1.7	21.6	19.6	9.5	−2.5	21.1

Ghana: 1960 = $534

1961–70	−1.4	n.a.	−1.6	n.a.	54.0	568	0.6	12.2	14.8	2.1	n.a.	11.5
1971–6	−11.8	−7.8	1.8	20.0	55.0	463	−3.3	21.7	10.8	14.3	−0.2	11.4
1977–82	−32.8	−8.4	−12.9	18.2	637.1	371	−3.6	67.9	5.7	1.4	−0.3	5.5
1983–8	−16.0	−1.0	8.2	15.3	191.8	368	−0.1	41.0	8.1	6.6	−1.2	5.9

Korea, Rep. of: 1960 = $690

1961–70	10.4	n.a.	6.6	n.a.	26.3	1189	5.5	12.5	19.9	33.4	n.a.	15.2
1971–6	0.0	−1.5	10.4	17.9	6.8	2013	9.1	15.3	26.1	38.6	−5.8	19.3
1977–82	−0.5	−2.2	10.0	13.7	7.0	2521	3.8	16.5	31.2	17.7	−5.5	26.5
1983–8	5.8	−0.2	6.1	13.0	2.8	4183	8.8	3.5	29.4	16.3	2.6	33.2

Mauritius: 1960 = $1012

1961–70	3.9	n.a.	−3.2	n.a.	n.a.	1025	0.1	2.7	16.3	2.4	n.a.	12.3
1971–6	−5.3	−5.2	13.8	18.0	n.a.	1552	7.2	13.9	25.8	29.3	1.7	22.3
1977–82	−5.3	−12.0	2.5	16.4	n.a.	1629	0.8	16.2	26.0	4.9	−10.2	16.3
1983–8	4.8	−3.0	−0.6	13.5	5.6	2125	·4.5	5.1	22.7	19.1	−0.6	23.4

cont'd

Table 1.2. Continued

	Measures of Government Intervention					Measures of Economic Performance						
	Real Interest Rate[b] (%)	Fiscal Surplus to GDP[c]	Real Growth Gov't Exp.[d] (%)	Gov'l Capital Exp.[e]	Exchange Premium (%)[f]	Real GDP per capita[g]	Growth GDP per capita[h]	Inflation (CPI)[i] (%)	Invest. Ratio to GDP[j]	Export Growth[k] (%)	Current Account Surplus[l]	Savings Rate to GDP[m]
Thailand: 1960 = $688												
1961–70	n.a.	n.a.	11.2	n.a.	1.2	1063	4.4	2.3	21.8	5.7	n.a.	21.4
1971–6	3.5	−2.2	6.1	22.2	−0.4	1384	4.5	8.8	25.0	25.3	−2.0	22.6
1977–82	−0.1	−4.4	11.5	23.6	−0.4	1730	3.8	10.4	26.4	15.7	−5.8	21.2
1983–8	7.2	−3.2	2.5	17.5	1.6	2269	4.6	2.5	25.0	13.8	−3.3	22.8
Turkey: 1960 = $1255												
1961–70	3.5	n.a.	12.3	n.a.	43.2	1702	3.1	3.7	16.7	5.9	n.a.	16.6
1971–6	−7.9	−1.7	8.8	2.8	4.8	2455	6.3	4.6	19.7	20.1	−2.1	16.3
1977–82	−19.5	−4.0	13.0	26.9	19.9	2397	−0.4	49.3	22.1	19.4	−3.7	16.0
1983–8	1.7	−5.4	3.3	20.6	6.3	2775	2.5	44.9	19.1	11.9	−1.7	19.9
Zambia: 1960 = $740												
1961–70	−1.5	n.a.	12.9	n.a.	19.0	789	0.6	4.3	24.1	5.9	n.a.	45.5
1971–6	−4.4	−12.3	4.0	17.5	92.0	918	2.7	9.0	33.8	−0.4	−7.1	35.5
1977–82	−6.6	−14.4	1.5	11.3	91.0	695	−4.5	14.0	20.4	2.7	−10.8	16.6
1983–8	−18.1	−11.5	−3.3	15.1	44.7	518	−5.7	37.1	15.1	1.0	−10.6	16.0

a All columns except real GDP per capita are expressed as averages over the period. Real GDP in 1960 is shown after each country name.

b Nominal deposit rate deflated by consumer price index.

c Fiscal surplus as a percent of nominal GDP.

d Growth of government expenditure deflated by GDP deflator.

e Capital component of government expenditure as a percent of nominal government expenditure.

f Percentage difference between the black market and official exchange rate.

g Real GDP per capita measured in 1985 US dollars at end of period, from Summers and Heston (1988) augmented by IMF statistics.

h Growth of real GDP using Summers and Heston data, augmented by IMF statistics.

i Inflation rate as measured by the consumer price index.

j Ratio of investment to nominal GDP.

k Growth rate of exports, measured in nominal US dollars.

l Current account surplus measured as a percent of nominal GDP.

m Savings rate measured as a percent of nominal GDP.

n.a. Not available.

Where data covering all years are incomplete, figures show averages of available data.

Sources: International Monetary Fund, International Financial Statistics, Yearbook (Washington, DC), 1990; International Monetary Fund, Government Financial Statistics (Washington, DC), 1990; Robert Summers and Alan Heston, "A New Set of International Comparisons of Real Product and Price Level: Estimates for 130 Countries, 1950–85," Review of Income and Wealth, Series 39 (1), March 1988; Adrian Wood, "Global Trends in Real Exchange Rates: 1960–84," World Bank Discussion Paper No. 35, 1988; World Bank, World Tables (Washington, DC), 1989–90; World Currency Markets (formerly Picks Currency Yearbook) (Washington, DC), 1989.

economic policies to slow down: Turkish economic growth
turned negative in the late 1970s, and Zambia's did so in an
even more pronounced fashion, reaching an estimated negative 5.7 percent per capita growth by 1983–8. By contrast,
countries such as Botswana, Korea, and Thailand, whose
policies appear to have been less unrealistic, sustained their
economic growth to a considerably greater extent. Second,
some countries managed – at least through the period covered
– to maintain positive economic growth at a cost of rising
inflation: the Brazilian case is the most prominent. There, by
the late 1980s, Brazilian inflation rates were triple-digit,
although real per capita income was growing. That Brazilian
growth was unsustainable given the policy stance of the late
1980s seems unquestionable.

Tables 1.3 and 1.4 present the same sort of data for 20
countries organized in a different way. Countries are divided
into three groups, based on their economic policies at different
periods of time. Thus, Turkey's policy performance was
judged to be poor during the period 1978–80, so Turkey was
placed during that period in the poor performance category.
By contrast, Turkey had undertaken extensive policy reforms
by 1982, so Turkey is placed in the reform period during
1982–8. Finally, some countries are deemed to have had
strong overall economic performance; and they are in
group 3.

Then, indicators of economic policy and of performance
were calculated for the periods indicated in tables 1.3 and
1.4. In addition to some of the indicators used in table 1.2
(real interest rate, fiscal surplus, the growth of real government expenditures, and the degree of exchange rate
overvaluation), table 1.3 gives the percentage of the total
government budget allocated to education. It is interesting to
note that educational expenditures, as a percentage of the
budget, appear to differ far less than other expenditures. In
light of the earlier-noted phenomenon, that most developing
countries appear to have made some progress with education
and health, the apparent lack of significant difference is interesting.

As can be seen, poor economic performance and poor policy again appear to be linked. The countries with the low rates of growth of per capita income (group 1) experienced an average negative real interest rate of almost 60 percent, while those countries undergoing reform averaged −1.7 percent and those with strong overall economic performance had a positive average real interest rate of 3.2 percent. Fiscal deficits averaged 7 percent for group 1 and 2.5 percent for group 3. Presumably because they were in the midst of a reform period, the group 2 countries averaged even smaller fiscal deficits – 1.5 percent of GDP – than did the group 3 countries. The indicator of restrictiveness of the trade and payments regime (column 6) is extreme – 419 percent – for countries with poor performance, and 5.1 percent for group 3 countries.

One other feature of the data in tables 1.2, 1.3, and 1.4 should be noted. That is, the good performers were exporting and growing in the same time period as the group 1 countries were in crisis: world economic conditions were largely the same for both groups of countries, and cannot be blamed for the difference in performance.

These statistical measures fail to capture many of the quantitative characteristics of policy failures, much less the qualitative ones. They nonetheless convey the degree to which negative real interest rates, overvalued official exchange rates, and fiscal deficits prevailed. They also provide an indication of the extent to which economic performance can respond and are strongly suggestive of the linkage between policy and performance.

4 Conclusions

In this lecture, I have tried to give an indication of the degree to which poor economic policy postures have occurred in developing countries. These postures have resulted in fiscal deficits many times the size of those encountered in developed countries; they have led to quadruple, and occasionally even quintuple, digit rates of inflation; they have led to declining

Table 1.3. Indicators of Policy Stances, Selected Countries and Periods

Country	Period	Real Interest Rate[a]	Fiscal Surplus to GDP[b]	Real Growth Govt Exp.[c]	Govt Capital Exp.[d]	Education Exp.[e]	Exchange Premium[f]
Group 1: Poor overall performance							
Argentina	1981–5	−40.9	−8.1	4.0	9.7	7.4	34.3
Bolivia	1980–5	−273.9	−16.4	15.5	4.5	20.6	199.3
Brazil	1981–3	−29.4	−3.0	6.7	6.3	4.1	37.6
Chile	1971–3	n.a.	−10.0	n.a.	n.a.	n.a.	1534.2
Ghana	1981–2	−35.4	−7.1	−3.9	13.5	17.9	1498.5
Nigeria	1981–4	−9.3	−4.2	25.2	n.a.	n.a.	154.2
Peru	1983–8	−105.0	−3.0	−6.3	17.1	16.8	28.1
Tanzania	1980–8	−17.3	−6.9	−1.5	n.a.	12.0	259.5
Togo	1980–3	0.8	−2.9	−8.4	27.3	19.7	n.a.
Turkey	1978–80	−76.0	−4.2	−3.3	26.0	17.7	28.1
Zambia	1977–87	−12.8	−13.2	−2.5	10.2	13.7	n.a.
Unweighted average		−59.9	−7.2	2.6	14.3	13.0	419.3
Group 2: Reform periods							
Brazil	1968–74	−3.4	−0.1	11.9	11.4	7.0	13.6
Chile	1976–88	8.7	0.3	2.6	10.3	13.8	14.8
Ghana	1985–8	−17.0	−0.3	14.5	17.7	22.9	107.1
Turkey	1982–8	5.4	−5.4	3.8	20.6	11.7	5.5
Unweighted average		−1.7	−1.4	8.2	15.0	13.9	35.3

Group 3: Strong overall performance

		[a]	[b]	[c]	[d]	[e]	[f]
Botswana	1980–8	−2.1	9.2	13.1	21.4	19.0	n.a.
Colombia	1980–8	5.4	−2.6	4.6	23.1	19.6	9.0
Indonesia	1980–8	0.2	−1.7	5.8	42.0	9.2	5.3
Korea	1980–8	3.1	−1.2	0.6	12.9	18.7	5.6
Malaysia	1980–8	5.1	−10.2	4.5	21.4	18.5	0.0
Mauritius	1980–8	0.7	−6.1	−0.2	11.5	14.7	n.a.
Pakistan	1980–8	3.4	−6.8	−2.4	11.9	2.4	16.8
Singapore	1980–8	3.0	1.4	12.3	23.7	18.6	0.0
Thailand	1980–8	6.9	−3.8	5.7	19.2	19.7	−1.3
Unweighted average		3.2	−2.5	4.9	20.8	12.8	5.1

[a] Nominal deposit rate less GDP deflator (bank rate for Brazil and Thailand).

[b] Fiscal surplus as a percent of nominal GDP.

[c] Growth of central government expenditure plus lending less repayments deflated by GDP deflator.

[d] Capital component of government expenditure as percent of nominal central government expenditure.

[e] Education component of government expenditure as percent of nominal central government expenditure.

[f] Percentage difference between the black market and official exchange rate.

n.a. Not available.

All columns are expressed as averages over the period. Where data covering all years are incomplete, figures show averages of available data.

Sources: International Monetary Fund, *International Financial Statistics, Yearbook* (Washington, DC), 1990; International Monetary Fund, *Government Financial Statistics* (Washington, DC), 13, 1989; *World Currency Markets* (formerly *Picks Currency Yearbook*) (Washington, DC), 1989.

Table 1.4. Indicators of Macroeconomic Variables, Selected Countries and Periods

Country	Period	Real Growth GDP[a]	Inflation[b]	Investment Ratio[c] to GDP	Export Growth[d]	Current Account Surplus[e]	Savings Rate[f] to GDP
Group 1: Poor overall performance							
Argentina	1981–5	-2.1	322.6	17.5	0.9	-3.3	18.0
Bolivia	1980–5	-2.1	440.7	12.4	-3.3	-3.3	22.7
Brazil	1981–3	-2.4	114.4	19.3	2.8	-4.4	19.1
Chile	1971–3	0.5	117.8	9.2	-0.5	-2.9	9.4
Ghana	1981–2	-4.5	62.6	4.0	-16.7	-1.0	3.9
Nigeria	1981–4	-4.7	22.3	14.7	-17.8	-4.9	10.8
Peru	1983–8	0.3	156.0	21.1	-3.1	-2.6	23.6
Tanzania	1980–8	1.2	30.5	19.2	-6.3	-5.1	6.6
Togo	1980–3	-2.7	13.1	20.6	-9.4	-7.6	13.9
Turkey	1978–80	-0.5	69.0	22.5	18.4	-3.5	14.9
Zambia	1977–87	-0.2	11.0	18.4	-1.5	-10.7	16.5
Unweighted average		-1.6	123.6	14.5	-3.5	-4.5	14.5
Group 2: Reform periods							
Brazil	1968–74	9.9	20.5	26.0	25.1	-3.6	20.2
Chile	1976–88	4.1	38.0	14.1	12.3	-6.4	15.7

		a	b	c	d	e	f
Ghana	1985–8	5.3	26.0	10.0	17.7	−1.6	7.1
Turkey	1982–8	5.4	36.6	19.2	13.9	−1.4	19.5
Unweighted average		6.2	30.3	17.3	17.3	−2.8	15.6
Group 3: Strong overall performance							
Botswana	1980–8	10.8	10.7	32.9	14.0	7.1	23.7
Colombia	1980–8	3.3	23.2	19.8	4.8	−3.2	20.0
Indonesia	1980–8	5.5	9.9	28.0	2.5	−2.6	29.4
Korea	1980–8	8.4	8.4	29.5	16.8	−0.3	30.4
Malaysia	1980–8	5.3	3.7	30.8	7.4	−3.3	32.9
Mauritius	1980–8	3.3	10.4	22.2	11.5	−3.5	20.1
Pakistan	1980–8	6.7	7.2	18.7	9.1	−11.3	9.4
Singapore	1980–8	7.0	2.3	43.8	11.9	−3.2	n.a.
Thailand	1980–8	6.3	5.7	24.9	12.9	−3.4	22.0
Unweighted average		6.3	9.4	27.8	10.1	−1.9	23.5

[a] Annual growth of real GDP using 1985 prices.
[b] Annual growth in consumer price index.
[c] Average ratio of nominal investment to GDP.
[d] Average annual growth of exports, measured in nominal US dollars.
[e] Current account surplus measured as a percent of nominal GDP.
[f] Gross domestic savings measured as a percent of nominal GDP.

All columns are expressed as averages over the period. Where data covering all years are incomplete, figures show averages of available data.

Sources: International Monetary Fund, *International Financial Statistics, Yearbook* (Washington, DC), 1990; World Bank, *World Tables* (Washington, DC), 1989.

production and exports of major exportable commodities, and to declining export earnings; and finally, but most importantly, they have resulted in falling standards of living for people who were already poor, in circumstances in which a stated major objective of policy was to raise living standards.

Obviously, in these circumstances, policy reform is called for. The policies of the typical developing country described above are unsustainable, even though they deliver poor and deteriorating results. The questions as to how the impetus for policy reform arises, what the issues are, and what is entailed are the subject of the next lecture.

2

Lecture Two
Economic and Political Issues in Formulating Reform Programs

In the first lecture, I showed how the economic policies chosen by a large number of countries had inevitably led to a deceleration of growth over time. Although this deceleration was sometimes postponed by increasing the rate of factor accumulation, by good fortune in the terms of trade, or by borrowing from abroad, it could not usually be indefinitely delayed. Without policy changes, real incomes and living standards would eventually have begun to decline, and in many sub-Saharan African countries that happened. In most other instances, however, an "economic crisis" typically arose and forced action before actual falls in income took place.

Regardless of the precipitating factors, a large number of governments have by now undertaken reform programs.[1] These programs have ranged from gradual alteration of a variety of policy instruments with little preannouncement, as in Colombia in 1967, to announcements of sweeping reforms to be implemented immediately, with other measures following, as in Turkey in 1980. A number of programs have been announced with great fanfare, where political opposition or

1 See table 2.1 later in this lecture.

other events have forced reversal within a short period of time. There have been programs which were manifestly failures and therefore implicitly abandoned within several months. Some programs have achieved their short-term objectives over a period of months or years, after which policies returned to their former stances. There have been programs which started haltingly but appeared to gain momentum with the passage of time. Some have resulted in far-reaching transformations of the structure of economic policy and the resulting incentives for economic activity. Others have not been intended to, and have not led to, longer-run change in economic policies, but have ameliorated the short-term difficulties that prompted the reform program.

It should go without saying that a failed reform episode has extremely high economic costs. Not only is there usually a period of slow growth, or even declines in output in the initial phase of the reform effort but, in addition, when reform programs fail, future living standards of poor people will arguably be considerably below those that would have been achievable had the reform program succeeded. Moreover, a failed policy reform effort increases the obstacles that will confront policy makers in the future when they contemplate reform programs: one key factor affecting the prospects for reform is the credibility of the program and peoples' assessments of the likelihood that the new policy measures will be sustained. To the extent that previous reform efforts have been inaugurated with optimistic pronouncements about the prospects for success, yet another such set of announcements will understandably be greeted with, at best, a wait-and-see attitude.

Despite the importance of insuring the success of a well-designed reform program, the sad fact is that more programs have failed than have succeeded, even partially.[2] A number

2 Vittorio Corbo and Stanley Fischer, *Adjustment Programs and Bank Support: Rationale and Main Results*, World Bank, CED Working Papers, WPS 582, January 1991, p. 4. A simple count of "successes" and "failures" is, however, unfair. Argentina had, as already mentioned, eleven "failures" while Korea really had only one "success." A truly successful reform obviates the need for further reforms of

of factors intrinsic in the necessity for reform are largely responsible for this record, and will be analyzed below. However, it seems clear that in some instances, a lack of understanding of the challenges of reform on the part of those designing the reform program contributed to failure. Another contributing factor on occasion has been opposition to reform programs, based at least in part on misconceptions about the necessity of reforms and/or the alternatives to reform. An effort to examine reforms, their difficulties, and what may be expected may, it is hoped, contribute to the success of future reform efforts, and thus to higher living standards.

A number of issues arise in the design and implementation of policy reform programs. I shall start with a very brief description of the nature and extent of policy reform efforts that have been undertaken. Thereafter, a natural next step is to consider the initial conditions in which policy decisions are made, and the crucial role of credibility. Next, attention turns to those aspects of policy, discussed in the first lecture, which normally require alteration, and to the interactions between them in designing reform programs. A fourth topic is then the question of "how much and how fast," which is closely related to the problem of attaining credibility. The fifth is the role of outside agencies and creditors in the design and support of policy reform efforts. A final aspect relates to the role of outstanding debt in the heavily indebted countries.

It will be observed throughout the discussion that a number of political issues and questions arise. In fact, in many instances policy reform programs fail, or at least are more costly than need be, because of the infeasibility of undertaking some of the necessary measures. Improved understanding of the political motivations and constraints that affect the choice of economic policies is highly desirable, both for its own sake,

---

the type discussed here, whereas failure usually results in the need for another effort at a later date.

and because it will permit more satisfactory formulation of future policy reform efforts. That subject, however, is deferred until the third lecture.

1 Reform Episodes

Definitions

What is a Reform Program?   A difficulty that arises in considering reforms is in formulating a criterion for when there was a "policy reform" program or effort. The difficulty arises in part because political leaders' announcements of their intentions are not a reliable indicator. In some instances, a "reform program" has been announced, but was not really such a program. In other cases, a set of measures, not billed as reform, constituted a genuine reform episode despite the absence of the label. In some instances, political leaders have reluctantly undertaken measures insisted upon by the multilateral lending institutions as a condition for eligibility for loans; it would appear that there was little, if any intention to change overall economic policies, and that the program was abandoned as soon as possible after loans were received.[3]

---

3 The Egyptian devaluation of 1963 is a classic in this regard. The authorities' commitment to maintaining existing incentives went so far that Hansen concludes that existing taxes and subsidy rates were altered by amounts just about sufficient to offset the change in the exchange rate in almost every sector of the economy! While that case is far-reaching, there is considerable evidence in many other cases that the authorities were not persuaded of the need for policy change, and undertook policy changes only to obtain IMF and World Bank loans. Adnan Menderes, then the Prime Minister of Turkey, appears to have been adamantly opposed to IMF-recommended changes, and undertook them only after imports of such vital commodities as petroleum (for which there was no domestic source) had ceased (discussed later). On Egypt, see Bent Hansen, *Foreign Trade Regimes and Economic Development, Egypt*, Columbia University Press (New York), 1975. On Turkey, see Anne O. Krueger,

In other instances, one reform program has no sooner failed than another was announced. It was mentioned earlier that Argentina has announced eleven reform programs in the past three years! While that country's difficulties are perhaps extreme, Brazil's numerous programs, Senegal's several efforts, and the track record of many other countries all attest to the frequency with which one reform program, after failing, is followed by another.

To ignore the failures would not only be unwise in its own right, but the record indicates that, even in cases of apparent longer-term success in reforms, the first such effort was not necessarily an outright success. Spain, for example, embarked upon a stabilization program in 1957 which was unsuccessful, only to adopt another one the following year which marked the beginning of Spain's rapid development. Even Chile, which from the perspective of the 1990s reforms are judged to have been largely successful, can be said to have had two distinct reform episodes – one (1974–81) in the early years of the Pinochet regime, and the second starting in 1984 or 1985 as the debt crisis was surmounted.[4]

Sometimes changes are made only reluctantly as a necessary condition for obtaining external credits; in those cases, they are seldom much more than cosmetic, and another "crisis" and/or the return of long-run stagnation sets in fairly quickly. In other situations, policy changes are sufficiently ameliorating so that moderate growth can resume after a period of adjustment. Finally, in a few cases, changes can be sufficiently far-reaching so as to alter the longer-term economic prospects of the country in question.

For purposes of these lectures, the concept of a "policy

Foreign Trade Regimes and Economic Development, Turkey, Columbia University Press (New York), 1975.

4 See Philip Brock and Barbara Stallings, "The Political Economy of Chile's Economic Reform Programs", in Robert H. Bates and Anne O. Krueger (eds), *Political and Economic Interactions in Economic Policy Reform Programs: Evidence from Eight Countries*, Basil Blackwell (Oxford), forthcoming.

reform program" is used to mean a set of policy changes that are announced and intended to be implemented to correct long-run difficulties in the overall functioning of the economy. Emphasis here is on the *set* of policies subject to reform. Normally, this would include monetary policy, alterations in government expenditures and tax policies to alter the fiscal balance and to change incentives to private actors (and often also to public actors) within the economy, and changes in the exchange rate and liberalization of the trade regime. In many instances, financial market and labor market liberalization might be involved, as well as changes in policies regarding activities of public sector enterprises and subsidies to private sector activities, most notably agriculture.

Thus, a "tax reform" might be very important for increasing government revenue and thus improving the fiscal balance, and also for altering incentives for economic activity, and then it might constitute an important part of a policy reform program. Another tax reform might be a stand-alone measure which was undertaken to improve the administration of taxes, or to improve the efficiency of resource allocation by moving to a more neutral tax structure. In the latter case, it would not be part of a policy reform program.

Likewise, adjustments in the exchange rate taken by themselves, as part of a "crawling peg" policy for example, would not constitute a policy reform. But an exchange rate adjustment, undertaken in conjunction with other measures designed to liberalize the trade regime as well as to reduce the magnitude of the current account deficit, would be part of such a program, if markets other than those dealing in foreign transactions were also involved.

Obviously, this definition of a policy reform program does not permit precise criteria by which to determine when a program is, and when it is not, a policy reform program, and an element of judgment is called for. Fortunately, however, most of the programs of the 1980s (and many earlier programs) have involved policy changes in a number of sectors of economic activity, and have been widely recognized as overall reform efforts. Moreover, identification of reform programs is, in practice, easier than definition because there are, with few exceptions, three situations in which policy reform programs are undertaken. These were (and are): (1) programs which in effect are in response to perceived emergency conditions, where the intent of the reformers is largely to mitigate the crisis conditions; (2) programs which respond to perceived emergency conditions, where the reformers intend to make fundamental alterations in the underlying structure of economic policy; and (3) programs which come about in a noncrisis atmosphere, usually because a change in government has resulted in altered perceptions regarding the effects of prevailing economic policies but occasionally for other reasons.

An example of each type may illustrate. The Egyptian program of 1963, for example, best fits the first situation described, as balance of payments difficulties impelled Egyptian officials to seek emergency support from the IMF, which could not be obtained without some changes in policy. As Hansen has documented, the Egyptian authorities were committed to their existing policies and proceeded to devalue the currency, but then added and removed taxes and subsidies to minimize the impact of the devaluation on domestic prices.[5] The Turkish programs of 1958 and 1970, the Indian devaluation of 1966, and the "stop–go" policies of Latin America also fit the first category. In all these (and many other) instances, a perceived shortage of foreign exchange and/or a high and accelerating rate of inflation was the emergency condition that triggered policy changes.

It has already been mentioned that Mexico spurred interest in the entire problem of developing countries in August 1982 when she announced that voluntary debt-servicing would no longer be possible. This was clearly a situation in which action had to be taken: failing to honor debt-servicing commitments was itself an action which would occur if nothing else was done. In fact, the Mexican authorities regarded the penalties for

5 Hansen, *Foreign Trade Regimes and Economic Development, Egypt*, chapter 4.

unilateral failure to honor commitments too great relative to their alternatives. In the Mexican case, oil revenues had increased rapidly both because of increases in the price of oil and because of newly discovered oil fields: the Mexican authorities recognized that large fiscal deficits had contributed to the problem, and stated, at the outset, that they intended to make fundamental changes in economic policy. This clearly included the magnitude of government expenditures, changes in the tax regime, an alteration in the exchange rate, changes in the trade regime (and especially a move away from quantitative restrictions), and a number of other measures. Some of these were undertaken immediately after the August 1982 announcement; others were taken in subsequent years. The Mexican policy reform program, therefore, was clearly an instance of an announced set of reforms which were designed to make fundamental alterations in the structure of economic policy that were precipitated by a crisis. The Korean policy changes of the early 1960s, the Turkish reforms of the early 1980s, the Indonesian changes following the 1966 revolution, and the Chilean policy reforms of the mid and late 1970s are also examples of the second type of reforms. In these instances, the commitment of the chief decision makers was to alter the underlying structure of the economy as well as to ameliorate existing economic conditions.

The third type of change – undertaken in a noncrisis situation – is harder to identify, in part because changes can be and often are more gradual, and in part because they are less dramatic. However, after the Sri Lankan election of 1977, a new government came into office with a mandate to dismantle the existing system of controls over economic activity and to shift toward a more market-oriented economy. There was considerable liberalization of the economy in the subsequent months, and the Sri Lankan reforms would therefore appear to be of the third type. There also appears to have been a shift in Colombian economy policy early in 1967 that was the result of decisions made by the Colombian administration in a noncrisis atmosphere.[6]

6 For a description, see Carlos Diaz Alejandro, *Foreign Trade Regimes and Economic Development: Colombia*, Columbia University Press, (New York), 1975.

Thus, most policy reform programs are normally at least in part identifiable because of the problems they are intended to address. When response is to crisis conditions, it may be difficult to discern whether decision makers genuinely desire change or not, but that policies are altered in response to the crisis situation is usually evident.

Duration of the Reform Program Some economic policies can be altered immediately, others can be changed relatively rapidly, while, for still others, changes take time to effect and even longer to implement.[7] Partly for that reason, but partly because programs evolve, policy reform packages are not announced and effected instantaneously. Questions therefore arise as to the time period during which a country's economic policies are subject to the reform process.

In instances where subsequent economic events clearly signal the failure of reforms, there is no difficulty in dating a reform episode. More often, however, there is no such definitive failure and judgments as to the end of the program must be somewhat arbitrary. This is the case, both with stabilization programs (especially for countries caught in stop–go cycles, discussed later in this lecture) where the

7 Policies which are subject to administrative conrol and which are of a "preventive" nature are subject to much more rapid alteration than are policies which require legislative action and an administrative staff to carry out. Thus, the exchange rate can usually be changed by decree, and import licensing can be substantially liberalized by increasing the quantity of foreign exchange available for license. Removing the import regime, minimum wage legislation, regulations surrounding employment or interest rate ceilings may require legislation, which takes somewhat longer. Implementing a value added tax system to replace existing taxes requires still longer: not only must legislation be prepared and passed, but the procedures for administering tax collection must be developed and staff put in place. In some cases, bureaucratic inertia or resistance may perpetuate controls even when the central government authorities have declared those controls no longer in effect.

objective was only to ameliorate existing crisis conditions, and especially with longer-term reform programs which successfully make fundamental alterations in the economy.

Consider, for example, the Korean reforms of the late 1950s and early 1960s. Korean economic policy in the mid 1950s was representative of the sorts of policies described in the first lecture. All imports were licensed, and there were multiple exchange rates; there were constant balance-of-payments difficulties despite substantial foreign aid. Inflation was rapid, and the government's deficits were substantially larger than the aid inflows. In an effort to curb inflation, the country undertook a stabilization program in 1957–8, which resulted in a reduction in the rate of inflation and a slowdown in the rate of economic growth. In 1960, there was a large devaluation, and export incentives were henceforth adjusted to maintain relative constancy in the real returns to exporters. Inflation, however, accelerated. In the early 1960s, many quantitative restrictions on imports were converted to tariffs. In 1964, there was a major fiscal reform which greatly reduced the size of the government's deficit; simultaneously, interest rate ceilings were relaxed and the exchange rate regime changed to a crawling peg. Indeed, one could continue the list of reforms to the present day, as there was further liberalization of the financial sector, of the trade regime, and of capital controls. Indeed, liberalization of imports and removal of tariff and nontariff barriers continues to this day.

Most observers, however, would date the period of reform as being in the late 1950s and early 1960s. Some would argue for 1957–60, including the first stabilization. Others would argue for 1960–3, the period during which the incentives for exports were stabilized, and some would pinpoint the 1963–4 reforms. Finally, some would include the entire 1957–64 period.[8] After that time, policy changes were made

8 See Suh, Suk Tai, "Import Substitution and Economic Development in Korea," mimeo, Korean Development Institute, 1975, for the argument that 1957–8 was the start of the reform period. Anne O. Krueger, in *The Development Role of the Foreign Sector and Aid*,

at various times, but the main outlines of overall policy – an outward orientation with strong incentives for exporters and a commitment to growth through trade – had been set.

Other successful reforms have had similar characteristics: there has been a period during which the fundamental policy stance has been altered, followed by further measures reinforcing those changes at later dates. The reform period, per se, however, is normally regarded as the period of alteration of the fundamental stance. For present purposes, a precise definition is not essential. What is significant is that there is typically a period of time during which reforms are being implemented, and during which there is a considerable basis for doubt as to whether the policy changes will endure over the medium term. That period ends either when the reforms are sufficiently widely accepted (normally because they have started to bring perceptible economic benefits) or when it becomes clear that the former policy regime is returning.

Thus, a policy reform program, by its nature, does not occur at a moment of time. For a successful reform, it normally spans several years. The phenomenon under discussion is, therefore, a process of policy change, and time is one of its ingredients.

Stop–Go Cycles   It has already been seen that reform programs have been undertaken in which there was little or no apparent intention to change significantly underlying economic policies, including import substitution, controls over private economic activity, and large-scale government involvement in production activities. In many of these instances, an apparent cycle developed. Known as the "stop–go" cycle, it was a sufficiently frequent experience among the developing countries to warrant some discussion.

Harvard University Press (Cambridge, MA), 1979, argues that the reform period was centered on 1960. Richard Cooper and Stefan Haggard, "Policy Reform in Korea", in Bates and Krueger, *Political and Economic Interactions in Economic Policy Reform Programs* place the reform period centering on 1963–4.

A stylized description will suffice. The starting point of the description of the cycle might be anywhere, but a natural one is at a point when the balance of payments position (given existing levels of protection for domestic import-competing industries) is reasonably comfortable and when primary attention of the economics team is on accelerating growth.

In such a circumstance, decisions are/were typically made to increase government investment and to liberalize the licensing of imports of raw materials and intermediate goods to permit increases in output in existing industries and imports of capital goods allowing expansion of those industries and the start-up of new import substitution activities. The real rate of growth of gross domestic product normally accelerates, but export earnings increase less than anticipated (or even fall) while the demand for foreign exchange for imports rises more sharply than anticipated. Inflation usually accelerates as investment expenditures exceed estimates, while tax revenues fall short of expectations. The authorities respond by tightening import licensing procedures and tightening credit to some extent, and the rate of economic growth may slow down. Even so, export earnings rise even more slowly, the foreign exchange necessary to meet liabilities incurred for imports and debt servicing obligations is greater than anticipated and met by rising foreign borrowing, and inflation continues. At some point, however, either the rate of inflation becomes politically unacceptable or foreign lenders will not extend additional credits to finance imports.

As import licenses are then restricted, economic growth slows down. Either the direct consequences of the import shortage or the consequent slowdown in growth finally becomes sufficiently unacceptable that the authorities approach the multilateral institutions, especially the International Monetary Fund (IMF) for support with their "balance of payment difficulties." When a program is worked out, several measures are implemented. These include adjustment of the exchange rate (which had often appreciated in real terms as the authorities maintained the nominal exchange rate despite inflation in an effort to control the rate of inflation), reductions in the government's fiscal deficit, and ceilings on the rate of credit expansion. Often, the domestic authorities accepted ceilings on credit, on the government fiscal deficit, and other measures in a letter of intent to the IMF.[9] Upon signing the document, the IMF would lend in support of the stabilization program, as such programs were typically called.[10]

Frequently, domestic economic activity would already have slowed down at the start of a stabilization program because of import shortages. However, cuts in government expenditures (or increases in tax receipts), tighter monetary conditions, and other aspects of the program would frequently lead to a further slowdown in economic activity. That, combined with the exchange rate devaluation, would usually result in a reduction in the demand for imports and an increase in export earnings. The resulting improvement in the current account position, and the increased foreign exchange reserve position resulting from receipt of the IMF loan and assistance from other official institutions, would then result in a relatively easy foreign exchange position accompanying

9 Stabilization programs undertaken with IMF support can entail a variety of other measures, depending on circumstances in individual countries. Very often, the IMF worked with national authorities to liberalize, if not dismantle, quantitative restrictions on imports. Changes were frequently called for in nominal interest rates so that they would be at least as high as the rate of inflation. Among other measures, less frequently encountered but often important, were removal of export taxes, increases in some sources of tax revenue, altered financing of parastatal enterprises and pricing of their products, and removal of subsidies to particular commodities (such as food) or sectors of the economy.

10 Often, the World Bank and bilateral donor agencies would also lend in support of stabilization programs. In some instances, "Donor Consortia" were established, with a "lead" institution. The leader was often the IMF or the World Bank, but it could also be the aid agency of one of the large donor countries which had a particular interest in the country in question. Representatives of the consortium would meet and review the prospective situation in the recipient country, and provide support in addition to the lending of the IMF.

slow economic growth (or even domestic recession). As that happened, the authorities would shift their attention to economic growth objectives, begin expanding government investment, and, in the context of relative ease of obtaining foreign exchange, expansion would resume and the cycle would restart.

The stop–go cycle was a frequent Latin American phenomenon, with Colombia, Uruguay, and Peru as well as Chile, Brazil, and Argentina all caught up in it. Chile underwent stop–go cycles during the 1950s and 1960s, with stabilization programs announced in 1956, 1959, and 1965. These cycles were much as described, with bursts of economic growth culminating in balance of payments and inflation difficulties, a reform program followed by recession, an improved balance-of-payments position, and thereafter renewed growth until the foreign exchange bottleneck once again emerged.[11] Many people identified the cycles themselves as a cause of slower growth than would otherwise have occurred. Indeed, Carlos Diaz Alejandro believed that a major reason for Colombia's more rapid economic growth after her policy reforms of 1967–8 was that the stop–go cycle was finally broken in that country.[12]

Stabilization and Structural Adjustment Programs   Until the 1980s, countries encountering balance of payments difficulties could approach the IMF and adopt a stabilization program, or they could themselves address their difficulties. The name "stabilization program" was consistent with an earlier-held view that the underlying conditions giving rise to balance of payments difficulties were unsustainable macroeconomic policies. Therefore, it was reasoned that underlying changes in macroeconomic policies would "stabilize" the situation, thus giving rise to the name. The IMF was the sole provider of support for these programs, as the World Bank was largely

11 See Jere R. Behrman, *Foreign Trade Regimes and Economic Development: Chile*, Columbia University Press (New York), 1975.
12 Diaz Alejandro, *Foreign Trade Regimes and Economic Development: Colombia*.

engaged in lending in support of development projects. Formally, these programs were generally "standby arrangements." Fund support generally lasted only for three years; the implicit theory was that the underlying causes of macroeconomic instability could be corrected within that length of time.

By 1980, however, it came to be recognized that balance-of-payments crises were occurring not only because of macroeconomic imbalances but also because of problems with the "underlying structure of the economy."[13] On one hand, the Fund increasingly provided loans for more than three years (EFFs and SAFs, the extended fund facility and structural adjustment facility).[14] On the other hand, the World Bank began granting "structural adjustment loans" (SALs) in support of policy reform programs. In addition to SALs, which were intended to provide support for overall policy reform, the Bank also engaged in sectoral adjustment loans, supporting policy reforms in specific sectors. These loans, known as SECALs, were normally intended to support reforms in such sectors as agriculture or trade, when there appeared to be little immediate prospect of overall reform but a significant probable payoff from removing costly and inappropriate policies in particular economic sectors.

By the mid 1980s, the IMF and the World Bank were both engaged in supporting policy reform efforts, and the dividing line between "stabilization" of macroeconomic policy and structural adjustment was sufficiently blurred that it was no longer a useful distinction. The World Bank continues to provide SALs and SECALs, and the Fund continues its activities with standbys, EFFs and SAFs (see table 2.1).

13 See Ernest Stern, "World Bank Financing of Structural Adjustment," in John Williamson (ed.), *IMF Conditionality*, Institute for International Economics (Washington, DC), 1983.
14 The SAF was later renamed the enhanced structural adjustment loan, or ESAF.

Table 2.1. Indication of Economic Policy Reform Programs in the 1980s (average)

	1970–9	1980	1981	1982	1983	1984	1985	1986	1987	1988	1989	1990	Total[a]
IBRD													
No. new SAL	—	3	6	6	7	6	3	7	13	10	7	7	5
No. new SEC	—	1	3	0	8	8	13	18	18	21	17	18	125
$US bill SAL & SEC	—	1	1	1	2	2	1	3	4	5	5	4	29
% total lending by IBRD	—	3	7	8	13	15	11	18	23	25	80	78	—
IMF													
No. new standbys, EEF & SAF	17	28	32	24	31	27	24	19	32	30	24	26	297
No. in effect	17	29	37	35	39	35	30	26	34	45	46	51	—
Value new initiatives[b]	1	3	10	11	14	4	3	3	5	3	5	11	72

% total outstanding credit	—	33	83	62	53	13	9	8	14	10	18	50	—
Debt rescheduling													
No. official	2	—	8	6	17	14	21	18	17	15	10	n.a.	126
No. commercial	1	—	5	4	27	26	14	11	17	8	0	n.a.	112
Value $US bill	2	—	5	2	56	96	40	84	121	92	12	n.a.	508

[a] 1980 to 1990; 1981 to 1989 for debt rescheduling.
[b] value in billions of Special Drawing Rights (SDR); 1 SDR in 1980 = $US1.30; 1 SDR in 1988 = $US1.34.
SAL Structural adjustment loans.
SEC Sectoral adjustment loans.
EFF Extended Fund Facility.
SAF Structural adjustment facility.
n.a. Not available.

Sources: World Bank, *World Debt Tables: 1988–9*, Vol. I and First Supplement; World Bank *Annual Report*, 1990; International Monetary Fund Annual Report, 1990; World Bank Special Report, "Lending for Adjustment: An Update," 1988.

Conditionality   As already noted, agreement between the IMF and a member country on a stabilization program was usually signified in a letter of intent from the President or Prime Minister of the country to the Fund. In many instances, Fund staff had reached the conclusion that certain policies had to be changed if there was to be any hope of returning to a viable balance of payments situation. In these circumstances, those policy changes were stipulated in the letter of intent, and the Fund typically declined to support programs until conditions judged at least minimally capable of bringing about the desired turnaround were agreed to.

These conditions became known as "conditionality": they were the conditions under which the Fund would lend, and the letter of intent then bound the government in the borrowing country to certain economic policies.[15]

Failures, Successes, and Mixed Outcomes   If there are problems defining when a reform program is undertaken, there are even more difficulties in determining the extent to which a program is successful. Fundamentally, the problem is that there are no known techniques with which to establish what would have happened in the absence of the program. Hence, judgment must be based on an assessment of what in fact happened.

There are a number of problems with forming such judgments. First, there are major difficulties in establishing what might have occurred in the absence of the program, especially where a simple continuation of existing policies was not a

15 For an exposition of the rationale for conditionality, see Manuel Guitian, "Fund Conditionality: Evolution of Principles and Practices," *International Monetary Fund Occasional Paper No. 38*, 1981. For reviews of Fund programs, see Thomas Reichmann and Richard Stillson, "Experience with Programs of Balance of Payments Adjustment: 1963–72," *International Monetary Fund Staff Papers*, Vol. 25, June 1978, p. 297. See also the collection of articles in John Williamson (ed.), *IMF Conditionality*, Institute for International Economics (Washington, DC), 1983.

plausible alternative. In a balance-of-payments crisis situation, for example, it cannot be assumed that imports would have continued to flow at the same rates that they did pre-reform: the alternative would clearly have been to have reduced imports still further and one question is: by how much? Secondly, there are always external changes impinging on a country. In some instances, terms of trade improvements may lead to a weakening of the reform effort, but with imperceptible results because of the offsetting gains in export earnings. In other instances, a drop in the prices of major export commodities after the start of a reform program may lead to drops in income which, in the absence of reforms, might have been even greater. But the analyst has no way of ascertaining what would have happened.

Because one cannot establish what would have happened in their absence, evaluation of the success of policy reforms must be undertaken on a different basis. Traditionally, it has been assumed that a major objective of developing countries has been the achievement of satisfactory rates of economic growth. As such, it has become traditional to use rates of economic growth as an indicator of the overall success or failure of reform programs.

Even with that indicator, however, there is serious ambiguity. As already noted, a period of declining economic activity often surrounds the inauguration of reforms. Growth rates in Turkey, which had been negative in the two years preceding the reform program, turned positive after 1980, but at relatively low rates. Only after 1985 did growth rates in excess of 5 percent – which most observers would regard as reasonably successful – occur. If, in addition, one examined the rate of export growth, which averaged more than 20 percent per year, the appearance of success was greater still. However, if, in addition, the inflation rate was taken into account, the picture was far murkier: from its high of more than 100 percent in 1980, the rate of inflation fell to around 30 percent in 1983, but thereafter rose again, reaching 70 percent in 1989.

The Turkish reforms are illustrative of a wider phenomenon: there are some elements of success, and some of failure. Even for successes and failures, there are longer or shorter intervals over which judgment must be made, and the picture is seldom clear. Nonetheless, in countries such as Korea, Chile, and Turkey, there is little question but that major changes in the structure of incentives and in the entire economic policy stance have occurred.

An Overview of the Numbers   Policy reform programs are not a new phenomenon in the 1980s, nor are they confined to developing countries. While many have failed, some of the successes have been spectacular. Indeed, in many instances, success has been so great that is is often forgotten that earlier economic conditions were far less satisfactory.

Perhaps the most striking example of this proposition is the West German "economic miracle," which started with major policy reforms that were introduced in 1948.[16] Less spectacular, but nonetheless very successful, were the programs undertaken in the mid and late 1950s by Finland and Spain. Finland, with support from the IMF, cut back public spending, altered the exchange rate, reformed the tax structure, and liberalized foreign trade in the mid 1950s, thereby ushering in a period of sustained growth and reasonable macroeconomic stability. Spain began a structural adjustment program in 1957 which failed, but then undertook major programs in 1958 which resulted in realigned incentives and an altered macroeconomic environment. The result was the start of a sustained period of more rapid economic growth which culminated, in the late 1980s, with Spanish entry into the European Community. In both of those instances, the result was a rapid acceleration in economic growth and reduction in the rate of

16 See Egon Sohmen, "Competition and Growth: The Lesson of West Germany," *American Economic Review*, 49 (4), 1959, pp. 986–1003.

inflation.[17] Also among the early successes that must be mentioned is Taiwan, whose economic policies were changed in the early 1950s, and Korea, whose economic reforms began in the late 1950s and continued into the 1960s.[18]

In later years, there were other reform efforts which have met with considerable success. In Indonesia after 1965, major policy reforms were instituted which reversed a rapid decline in output and living standards and inaugurated a period of successful economic growth.

But if there have been spectacular successes with policy reform, there have also been spectacular failures. Argentina's eleven reform programs in two years were already mentioned in the first lecture. In fact, however, reform programs in Argentina and many other countries date back to the 1950s. Brazil's cruzado plan of the mid 1980s, and subsequent Brazilian plans, have also had little, if any, impact on the course of inflation and other macroeconomic variables for any sustained period of time.[19]

More frequently, however, stabilization programs and other reform programs met with initial success in improving the current account and/or reducing the rate of inflation, but did

17 For an account of these reforms, see Ernest Sturc, "Stabilization Policies: Experience of Some European Countries in the 1950's," *International Monetary Fund Staff Papers*, July 1968, pp. 197–279.

18 On Taiwan, see S. C. Tsiang, "Foreign Trade and Investment as Boosters for Take-Off: The Experience of Taiwan," in Vittorio Corbo, Anne O. Krueger, and Fernando Ossa (eds), *Export-Oriented Development Strategies*, Westview Press, (Boulder, CO) 1980. On Korea, see Charles R. Frank, Kwang Suk Kim, and Larry E. Westphal, *Foreign Trade Regimes and Economic Development: Korea*, Columbia University Press (New York), 1975.

19 At the time of revising these lectures in the winter of 1990–1, the Collor Government in Brazil marked its first anniversary in office. During that year, inflation (which was the chief target of the initially announced policy reforms) ran at an annual rate of 400 percent, and reached a monthly rate of 21 percent in February 1991. See *New York Times*, March 14, 1991, p. A3.

not result in long-lasting changes.[20] The list of such programs is long.[21] To name just a few, in 1956, Argentina for the first of many times, and, in 1958, Turkey for the first of three efforts also undertook major stabilization, as they were then called, programs.[22] Hansen[23] shows that a 1963 program in Egypt had almost no effect on the structure of incentives or the role of government in the domestic economy, although the balance of payments situation did improve. Ghana's policy reforms of 1966 permitted resumption of growth for several years, but had no long-lasting effects on the structure of the economy or on incentives.[24]

The shakeout of the early 1980s changed all that, however. Table 2.1 (pp. 74–5) gives some indication of the number of

20 Carlos Diaz Alejandro was among the first to note that IMF-sponsored programs appeared to have been generally successful in producing significant alterations in the current account balance. See Carlos F. Diaz Alejandro, "Southern Cone Stabilization Plans," in William R. Cline and Sidney Weintraub (eds), *Economic Stabilization in Developing Countries*, Brookings Institution (Washington, DC), 1981.

21 See Reichmann and Stillson, "Experience with Programs of Balance of Payments Adjustment."

22 Information on these, and other, early reforms may be obtained from the International Monetary Fund's *Annual Report on Trade and Exchange Restrictions*, various years, and from Keith Horsefield, *The International Monetary Fund 1945–1965*, International Monetary Fund (Washington, DC), 1969.

23 Hansen, *Foreign Trade Regimes and Economic Development: Egypt*, reports that the Egyptian authorities undertook an IMF program in 1963 with great reluctance: they were anxious to obtain the proceeds of a loan and therefore agreed to a nominal devaluation of about 25 percent. However, as he demonstrates, the authorities managed to remove a sufficient number of surcharges on imports and subsidies for exports so that almost no exporters or importers were receiving or paying more than 3 percent more local currency per unit of foreign exchange than they had earlier.

24 See J. Clark Leith, *Foreign Trade Regimes and Economic Development: Ghana*, Columbia University Press (New York), 1975.

policy reform efforts in the 1980s. The first block relates to activities of the World Bank and the second to activities of the IMF. Although there were a few reform programs adopted without support of either institution, these numbers provide dramatic evidence of the increase in policy reform activity in the 1980s.

The World Bank had no SALs or SECALs in the 1970s. It started in 1980 with three SALs and one SECAL; by 1985 there were three SALs and 13 SECALs, and by 1988 there were 10 new SALs and 21 SECALs. If anything, the increase in IMF activity was even more dramatic: from an annual average of 17 new standbys and other lending arrangements in the 1970s, Fund activity rose to a peak of 31 new programs in 1983, with a total of 39 in effect, fell off somewhat, and then rose again to 32 new programs in 1987. Altogether, the Fund put 271 new programs in place in the 1980s! Since there are fewer countries than that, it is clear that some countries were recipients of more than one Fund-lending operation.

2 Conditions in which Reforms are Undertaken

In the next section, the content of policy change in reform programs is addressed. Before that, however, consideration must be given to the conditions under which most policy reforms are undertaken. It was noted earlier that the majority of policy reforms are initiated in what are perceived as crisis situations. Ideally, the determination of the overall economic policy framework should be the subject of political discussion and consensus. In crisis conditions, however, that is a difficult, if not impossible, situation, although there have been a few instances of policy changes brought about by changes in government. That happened in Sri Lanka in 1977 and in New Zealand in 1983, and in both circumstances the extensive role of government in the economy had been subject to intense debate during the preceding electoral campaign.

Apparent crises can take two forms, and either normally

results in circumstances in which decisions are taken quickly and by a small group. The first, and possibly more frequent, is when imminent difficulties in meeting foreign currency obligations trigger action.

In a deteriorating economic environment of the sort described in the first lecture, it is very frequently the disappearance of additional sources of foreign exchange that triggers the crisis. Typically, in the preceding period, the exchange rate has not been adjusted to keep pace with inflation, while import licensing has become more and more restrictive. Observers, noting the increased premium on black market foreign exchange, the failure of export earnings to keep pace with GNP, possibly intensified smuggling activity, and the mounting excess demand for imports, begin to withhold even traditional commodities from export channels in anticipation of a change in the exchange rate, while importers scurry to obtain imports before licensing becomes even more stringent and/or the exchange rate is altered.

Those expectations in themselves trigger capital flight, which further reduces the foreign exchange passing through official channels, and therefore the authorities' ability to finance legitimate foreign exchange transactions. In some cases, the speculative attack on the currency in itself is a triggering point for action: this has been true of developed countries as well as of developing countries. In those circumstances, the authorities are confronted with a situation in which foreign exchange received in official channels drops off sharply while the demands for foreign exchange mount rapidly.

Of course, in the short run, imports can be financed with suppliers' credits and other short-term high cost financing. But, once it is known that a country is in arrears even with regard to suppliers' credits, any additional funding disappears.

The Turkish situation in 1980, and the Mexican situation in 1982, illustrate the environment within which policy actions are taken. Turkey had had five years of accelerating inflation, which was the result of several factors including large fiscal deficits. These deficits resulted both from an excess of general government expenditures over revenues, and from the excess of expenditures over receipts of the state-owned enterprises. This latter number itself was in excess of 5 percent of GNP by 1980, in part because the authorities had denied permission for state-owned enterprises to raise their prices (because they knew that would increase the recorded rate of inflation). Despite several adjustments of the nominal exchange rate, the real exchange rate appreciated sharply in the late 1970s. Two stabilization programs, in 1977 and 1978, were announced but subsequently abandoned.

In these circumstances, delays in receiving import licenses increased sharply, so that many businesses were operating at far less than capacity, and even shut down for periods of time awaiting raw materials, intermediate goods, and spare parts. The black market exchange rate skyrocketed, while export earnings surrendered through official channels fell.

By the winter of 1979–80, the situation was clearly one of crisis. There were no imports of petroleum (which Turkey does not produce) due to lack of ability to finance them; that, in turn, meant not only that Turkish refineries were operating well below capacity but that trucks carrying coal (for heating) and agricultural commodities (which might have been exported if they could have been harvested and transported) were operating well below capacity. In a severe Anatolian winter, most buildings were without heat, and imported commodities such as coffee had simply disappeared from the shelves of most stores. It was even reported that Turkish employees in Turkish embassies abroad had not been paid for several months, simply for lack of foreign exchange.

Such a situation is clearly one of crisis. No additional funds can be obtained by borrowing until potential creditors believe that actions have been taken to correct the fundamental situation. Export earnings will not increase until actions are taken, and, indeed, continue to decline. There is also a partial or total loss of official control as more and more transactions take place outside official channels.

In Turkey, a very small team of officials worked in secret

to prepare a policy reform program. Even when information was needed from other governmental sources, it was requested in ways that did not permit those supplying it to infer what was happening. When the reforms were announced on January 25, 1980, it is estimated that less than ten people, including the President and the Prime Minister, knew the contents of the program, so great had been the surrounding secrecy.

The reform program of necessity included a large change in the nominal exchange rate. It also included measures such as large increases in the prices of the outputs of parastatal enterprises. Such changes cannot be the subject of prior public discussion, as people would accelerate their purchases of existing stocks of goods in anticipation of price increases and even greater pressures on the foreign exchange market would develop. To be sure, informed observers in such a situation can anticipate change and attempt to profit at existing prices, but public discussion would increase the frequency and intensity of such behavior.

The inability to carry out public discussion, which is inevitable, nonetheless has a number of consequences. First, there is often a negative public reaction because of the appearance of hardship as price increases are announced. Businessmen who are dependent on imports also object because their costs of inputs (when they can get them) are increased. Second, the team developing the plan normally is subject to considerable time pressure (as speculation mounts, and as foreign exchange vanishes) and must make decisions quickly. Third, decision makers must make choices without benefit of consultation with others who might be able to suggest preferable alternatives.

In Mexico in 1982, the crisis was equally acute, but had different antecedents.[25] Mexico as a major oil exporter directly benefitted from the oil price increase of 1979. The large size

25 There are a number of accounts of the events leading up to the Mexican crisis. One of the most readable is that of Joseph Kraft, *The Mexican Rescue*, Group of Thirty (New York), 1984.

and rapid growth of those exports gave commercial bank lenders confidence in Mexico's creditworthiness, to the point where syndicated loans were oversubscribed and banks were eager to increase their lending.

However, Mexicans, and especially Mexican politicians were equally informed about the oil bonanza, and pressures for increased governmental expenditures increased even more rapidly than did oil export revenues. Government expenditures rose more rapidly than revenues and, in the late 1970s and until the summer of 1982, additional credits from commerical banks financed the resulting fiscal and current account deficits. By the summer of 1982, however, the incipient fiscal deficit exceeded 17 percent of GNP, and inflation had been at rates well above those in Mexico's major trading partners while the exchange rate had remained pegged to the US dollar (which was, in any event, appreciating).

Consequently, it became evident to a number of observers that the situation was unsustainable, and capital outflows increased sharply. Within the period of eight months, starting December 1981, foreign exchange reserves fell from $US4.1 billion to $US1.3 billion.[26] By mid-summer, it was evident that Mexico could no longer voluntarily service her debt.

In the Mexican case, speculative capital outflows were already very large. However, public discussion of the authorities' dilemma would have been unthinkable, leading to even larger capital outflows. And, even more than in the Turkish case, speed was essential, both because of the size of the outflows and because failure to take action would inevitably involve default on outstanding debt, with major consequences for Mexico's ability to finance imports of goods and services.

With a balance-of-payments crisis, open discussion of alternative changes in the exchange rate – whether to devalue once-and-for-all, by how much to devalue, whether to adopt a crawling peg, what basket of currencies, if any, to peg to –

26 Data from International Monetary Fund, *International Financial Statistics*, May 1983, Mexico pages.

is simply infeasible. In principle, one could free the exchange
rate to float freely and then encourage open discussion of
alternative exchange rate policies, but, in practice, policy
makers are reluctant – at a time when foreign exchange
reserves are low, when capital flight is occurring, and when
excess demand for imports appears extreme – to permit a free
float in a crisis period.

In both the Mexican and the Turkish case, the underlying
difficulties were with domestic macroeconomic policy, but the
triggering circumstances that forced action lay in the foreign
exchange market. The majority of policy reform programs are
of that kind, but there are a few where the rate of inflation
itself is unacceptable and is the stimulus to reform. The
Bolivian reforms were undertaken when the rate of inflation
in that country reached an annual rate of 40,000 percent in
1984. Although the foreign exchange situation was serious,
it was clearly the inflation which created the crisis situation.
Similarly, some of the Argentina reform attempts have been
motivated more by political intolerance of inflation than by
foreign exchange considerations.

When inflation is the crisis event without immediate foreign
exchange difficulties, there can, at least in principle, be some
degree of public discussion of alternative monetary and fiscal
packages that might address accelerating inflation.[27] Alternative expenditure cuts and tax increases are often the stuff of
which political debate is made. Public discussion, however,
often results in pressures to reduce the anticipated increase
in tax revenues and the magnitude of cuts in public expenditures. One consequence can be that cuts are far smaller than
what professional analysis would indicate as necessary for the
reforms to be effective.

27 To be sure, there are also policy measures which, if discussed,
could invite profitable anticipatory behavior. For example, this was
certainly the case with the Brazilian decision, when President Collor
assumed office, to freeze all overnight deposits in excess of about
$1,000: had it been discussed as an option in advance, it is hard
to imagine how a run on the banks could have been avoided.

Whether foreign exchange difficulties or an unacceptably high rate of domestic inflation triggers the decision to undertake policy changes, the important fact is that either set of circumstances constitutes both a crisis situation and a circumstance in which information may not be fully available to the authorities. Officials are even more likely than usual to be caught up in day-to-day emergencies (including such mundane items as being beseiged by local businessmen who have an extremely urgent need for foreign exchange to replace one essential spare part or to provide one critical intermediate input and attempting to finance the latest month's scholarships to students studying overseas, but more frequently focussing on how to maintain debt-servicing obligations with each of a large number of creditors), which is not a circumstance in which long-range vision is at its best.

Nor are policy makers likely to feel that there is time for a considered judgment of alternatives and careful weighing of policy decisions. On top of that, such situations by their nature usually obscure a lot of economic information: how much short-term debt has built up, what the magnitude of foreign liabilities is, how much capital flight there has been, what domestic inventories are, and answers to a variety of other questions are even more subject to large margins of error than is normally the case. Furthermore, negative political reactions to the existing situation are inevitably strong, as almost all groups in society will find it easy to agree that the existing situation is undesirable, and to place blame for it on the government and the economic policy team.

Not only must officials, in these circumstances, decide that changes must be made, they must decide which instruments should be altered, and by how much. Moreover, the sorts of changes that are undertaken are seldom those that can be made – even by finance ministers or ministers of economy – without approval of the head of government, and often of the cabinet. In haste, and in a crisis atmosphere, the program must be sold to the relevant political masters.

Typically, when this has happened, economic officials of the country have approached the international institutions,

and sought their financial support. Discussions then progressed between the international institutions and those
officials, sometimes with consultation of a donor or donors
with special interests in the country. Once a program of
reform and the necessary financial support was agreed upon,
a Fund program would be put in place, often with additional
resources provided by major donor countries. Thereafter, the
country's officials would meet in Paris with official creditors,
for official debt rescheduling, and with commercial banks,
when commercial debt was also, as was often the case, to be
rescheduled. A Fund program, and often a Bank Structural
Adjustment Loan, were then in effect, with prenegotiated
ceilings on critical macroeconomic variables as conditions for
releases of the various Fund tranches, and various actions
agreed upon between Bank officials and the government in
question as preconditions for rapidly disbursing SALs and
SECALs.

All of the considerations cited make decision making
extremely difficult just at a point when it is critical. There
is yet one further complication: very often, dissatisfaction
with the economic situation prompts heads of governments to
appoint new ministers to head the economic program of the
government. These ministers assume their jobs in the midst
of crisis, and are caught doubly off-guard: on one hand, they
may be unfamiliar with their ministry and their job and, on
the other, they must act quickly or be seen to be ineffective
in carrying out their mandate to stem the crisis.

In these circumstances, it is small wonder that so many
policy reform programs have failed. This will become even
more evident as attention turns to the various components of
a policy reform package.

3 Policy Instruments Requiring Alteration

In a few instances, the circumstances that bring about the
decision for changes are concentrated on one key market. In
1966, for example, Indian officials were confronted with a

major balance of payments crisis. Indian fiscal and monetary policy had been reasonably conservative, and Indian inflation had not been unduly high by international standards. What had happened was that the initial exchange rate which had been set for the Pakistani and Indian Rupees was arguably overvalued. Pakistan had altered her nominal exchange rate a decade before India, which made Indian exports even less competitive in markets in which the two countries competed. Moreover, Indian decisions to accelerate investment in heavy industry and to encourage import substitution had shifted the demand for foreign exchange sharply outward. Simultaneously, export earnings were growing very slowly given the pull of resources into the highly profitable and heavily protected import-competing activities. The restrictiveness of the import licensing regime and the shortage of foreign exchange were demonstrably adversely affecting both the level of economic activity and growth prospects, and it was clear that the situation would deteriorate still further without action.[28]

While the crisis in the foreign exchange market had repercussions in virtually all Indian economic activities, the stabilization program could be designed essentially around changes in the trade and payments regime.

Circumstances such as that of India in 1966 are, however, the exception. For reasons outlined in the first lecture, in the overwhelming majority of cases there are a number of policies that are inimical to growth and unsustainable. Typically, foreign exchange difficulties trigger the crisis, and amelioration of that situation requires changes at a minimum in the trade regime, in the exchange rate, in exchange controls, and in monetary and fiscal policy. Thus, reforms in the macroeconomic policy stance and in the trade regime are

28 See Jagdish N. Bhagwati and T. N. Srinivasan, *Foreign Trade Regimes and Economic Development: India*, Columbia University Press (New York), 1975, for an account of the Indian devaluation, which was not a success.

fundamental, and probably the most important two sets of measures that need to be taken.[29] These two sets of measures, of course, encompass a large variety of policy actions, and are by no means simple.

Interactions between the trade and payments regime and macroeconomic policies are usually even more important in developing countries than they are in developed countries. Most developing countries started their drives toward development since World War II. When they began, the structures of their economies were highly specialized, with exports of a few primary commodities and imports of a wide variety of manufactured goods that were, at that time, not domestically produced. In 1950, the agricultural sector accounted for 70–80 percent of the "typical" developing country's population, and around half of its GNP. Exports consisted predominantly of agricultural commodities and minerals, with large fractions of agricultural and mineral outputs being exported.

The interdependence between developing countries' economies and the rest of the world was therefore pronounced. As incentives were provided through the trade regime for import substitution industrialization policies, the agricultural sector

29 In many developing countries, discrimination against agriculture has been of sufficient magnitude to provoke strong supply responses, and a migration of rural workers to the cities. In those circumstances, measures to stimulate agricultural production are a necessary condition for increasing export earnings and resuming growth. However, two of the main instruments of discrimination against agriculture in developing countries have been the overvaluation of the exchange rate and high tariffs (and quantitative restrictions) on imports of commodities purchased by farmers. Thus, an exchange rate adjustment that results in a depreciated real exchange rate and a less restrictive trade regime goes a long way toward reducing discrimination against agriculture. See Anne O. Krueger, Maurice Schiff, and Alberto Valdes, "Agricultural Incentives in Developing Countries: Measuring the Effects of Sectoral and Economywide Policies," *World Bank Economic Review*, 2(3), September, 1988, pp. 255–72.

diminished in importance: new industries were growing rapidly, and outmigration proceeded from rural areas.[30] Especially as growth tended to slow down, and the capital intensity of new investments increased, pressures were strong to increase the rate of investment. As that happened, inflationary pressures intensified, the real exchange rate appreciated, and there were still further disincentives for agricultural production.

In most developing countries, therefore, expansionary macroeconomic policies quickly resulted in an appreciating real exchange rate. Simultaneously, because those economies were relatively specialized and relied upon imports of many capital goods, "foreign exchange shortage" was seen to be the bottleneck to more rapid economic growth.

The linkages between macroeconomic problems and foreign exchange problems were therefore of the same general type as in developed countries, but they were and are tighter. Moreover, as will be argued in section 4, the extremely close relationship between macroeconomic variables and the trade and payments regime is the fundamental reason why both problems in domestic macroeconomic variables and in the trade and payments regime need to be addressed simultaneously in a policy reform program. Moreover, it is arguable that, in most cases, if policy reform successfully restores a sustainable macroeconomic and trade and payments framework, it will succeed, and other growth-inhibiting policies can be addressed subsequently (although this is not necessarily a reason for delay). If these reforms fail, it is likely to undermine the entire reform program.

In individual circumstances, however, there are other policies that require alteration if economic prospects are to have significant hope of improvement. In some instances, such as

---

30 With well-managed development, this same pattern would occur, but it would be largely a consequence of productivity increases in agriculture and thus happen in the context of rising agricultural exports and food output.

when parastatals are incurring large budget deficits or when food subsidies are a major drain on budgetary resources, these measures are related to macroeconomic stability and are discussed under that heading here. In other cases, however, policies not directly related to foreign trade and or macrostability are very important. These include such phenomena as pricing of agricultural commodities, reforming (or at least removing the government's monopoly over) the distribution system for agricultural inputs and outputs, and removing restrictive labor market legislation.

There are also a variety of longer-term measures that are often carried out in the months or years following the initiation of a reform program, which contribute to accelerated economic growth. These include such phenomena as improved effectiveness and efficiency of communications and transportation systems, privatization of activities earlier carried out by parastatals, and deregulation of economic activities.[31]

Because of their fundamental and far-reaching importance, I focus here on macroeconomic reforms and reforms in the trade and payments regime. Thereafter, there is a brief discussion of other measures which have been important in particular circumstances but which are not as universal nor as key to the success of reforms as the trade and payments regime and macro reforms are.

Throughout this section, focus is on the changes in policy

---

31 Some of the important reforms that have been undertaken in Chile include the privatization of the social insurance system, the modernization of the port system, privatization of some economic activities, removal of regulations giving workers job security in virtually all circumstances, and major reduction in regulation of food imports and distribution. These were *in addition* to the major alterations in the trade regime, the realignment of the real exchange rate, and the attainment of macroeconomic stability. See Vittorio Corbo and Andres Solimano, "Chile's Experience with Stabilization, Revisited," and the references cited therein, for particulars (World Bank Country Economics Department, Working Papers in Macroeconomic Adjustment and Growth, January 1991, WPS No. 579).

that are desirable for restoring macroeconomic equilibrium and growth in countries confronting the necessity for policy reform. I take it as given that the desirable outcome of reform programs is to achieve a policy stance which will permit more efficient resource allocation, and therefore be conducive to more rapidly rising living standards, especially of the poor. The record of success with these programs has not been as favorable as might have been hoped, so a central concern of these lectures is to understand why.

Monetary and Fiscal Measures

It is widely recognized that in most circumstances the root cause of rapid and accelerating inflation is an excess of governmental expenditures over receipts. Receipts, of course, include those from foreign aid and normal capital inflows that increase the resources available for the public sector on a sustained basis. Since foreign capital is normally available to finance activities with high economic and financial real rates of return, an excess of expenditures over receipts beyond the sustainable level usually implies that a considerable fraction of government expenditures are devoted to activities (including transfers) that have a very low productivity.

In some developing countries, the proximate motive for undertaking policy reform is an unacceptably high rate of inflation. That was certainly the case in Bolivia in 1983–4, and in Argentina and Brazil in their many unsuccessful reform efforts in the latter part of the 1980s. In many other instances, including Turkey in 1980, Chile in 1983, Mexico in 1982, and Ghana in 1983–4, inflation fuelled by large public sector deficits is a major contributing factor to balance of payments difficulties which spur reform programs.

By the time the necessity for policy reforms is normally confronted, options of additional domestic money creation and/or borrowing or of foreign borrowing have typically been exhausted, or, in rare instances, recognized as failing to address the fundamental problem. Usually, domestic borrowing has already resulted in a large domestic debt-service

burden and interest rates have risen to a point where interest
on the domestic governmental debt itself is a major source of
money creation. By 1987, for example, interest service on Mexican internal debt equalled 15 percent of GNP, and accounted
for 94 of the 147 percent increase in the money supply.[32]

Expenditure cuts and/or increases in tax revenues are therefore a necessary part of the program. And, while arguments
can proceed as to whether a fiscal deficit of 2–3 percent of
GNP is inflationary, there can be little disagreement about
fiscal deficits of the order of magnitude that these countries
had prior to reforms or that are indicated in table 1.2 of my
first lecture. They are inflationary, and often greatly so.
Whether inflation itself is the source of sufficient discomfort
to spur a program of reforms, or whether balance-of-payments
difficulties are the proximate motivation, almost all policy
reform programs have a large macroeconomic stabilization
component. When public sector deficits are large, and/or
inflation is proceeding at annual rates in excess of, say, 100
percent, major reduction in the size of the public sector deficit
is a virtual necessary condition for the success of the reform
effort.

How much the public sector deficit must be reduced is, to
a degree, a matter of judgment. When inflation is triple or
quadruple digit, and when previous efforts at reform have
failed, it is arguable that credibility of the reforms will be
weak unless the deficit is entirely eliminated. But, regardless
of the necessary magnitude of reduction in the public sector
deficit, a frequent cause of failure of policy reform is the
inability or unwillingness of the authorities to make sufficiently large expenditure cuts or revenue increases.[33]

---

32 Dwight S. Brothers and Adele E. Wick, *Mexico's Search for a New
Development Strategy*, Westview Press (Boulder), 1990.
33 The size of the necessary change can be reduced if arrangements
can be made for increased foreign aid. However, unless the flow of
foreign aid is expected to be continued over the intermediate run,
short-term assistance may not provide sufficient credibility as to the
sustainability of reforms.

Politically, taking steps to cut expenditures or raise revenues is difficult. Regardless of how low the social product of the expenditure in question may be, there are those who benefit from it, including at least those who receive the first round of payments. Those who stand to benefit from policy reforms will do so only at a later date (and may not know they will benefit). By contrast, the pain of losing governmental employment, contracts, or transfers is immediate. Resistance to expenditure cuts is naturally great, and politicians are sensitive to the fact that they will pay political costs for making them. Moreover, in the short run, the choices as to which expenditures to cut is difficult: investment projects are at varying stages of completion, some transfer payments are entitlements, and many government employees work for central ministries and really cannot be relieved of their duties.

There is an inevitable temptation to make across-the-board cuts, or else to cut investment and maintenance expenditures, protecting current consumption. The difficulties with this policy are several: (1) indiscriminate cuts in investment and maintenance result in subsequent pressures to resume an equally indiscriminate increase, if mechanisms are not put in place to rationalize public sector investment and maintenance at the time reforms are instituted; (2) very often, the greatest waste is in some public consumption expenditures and transfers, while maintenance often has a very high marginal product as do *some* public investments; and (3) since there are in any event doubts about the willingness of the government to continue the reform program, across-the-board cuts are normally interpreted as a sign that things will return to "normal" within a short time period, and individuals do not therefore respond to altered incentives which are taken to be short run.

Thus, a successful reform program entails immediate decisions as to how cuts should be selectively made. In some instances, some of the places where cuts should be made are fairly obvious: deficits of parastatal enterprises, as in Turkey in 1980; excess costs of food subsidy programs as in Egypt, Morocco, and Zambia; or "white elephant" investment projects in many countries. In other cases, establishing teams to undertake cost–benefit analyses and make selective cuts in public sector programs permits rationalization of expenditure programs. Moreover, there are some public sector expenditures that must be increased, if the reform is to achieve its desired goals. In Ghana, for example, maintenance work on communications and transportation facilities was essential in order to make increased volumes of exports feasible.[34]

Things are no better on the tax side: not only are tax increases politically unpopular, but they generally require legislation and take considerably longer to effect than do expenditure cuts.[35] Thus, if the government's fiscal deficit is to be substantially reduced in the short run, that will normally be accomplished largely by expenditure cuts.

Strong political resistance to expenditure cuts or tax increases does not prevent them, but it puts downward pressure on the size of the cuts/increases. Even when political leaders admit the necessity for policy reform, they will attempt to make the smallest cuts possible. "Political infeasibility" of

34 Joseph L. S. Abbey, *On Promoting Successful Adjustment: Some Lessons from Ghana*, The 1989 Per Jacobsson Lecture, Per Jacobsson Foundation (Washington, DC), September 24, 1989, p. 10. At the time of revising this manuscript, Nigeria and the multilateral agencies were attempting to agree upon a reform program. A major issue was Nigeria's proposed Ajaokuta Steel plan, which had cost more than $4 billion on construction in the 1980s and was not yet operational. The Nigerians proposed to complete the project for an estimated additional $2 billion, while officials of the multilateral organizations questioned the likely rate of return, especially given the need for expenditure reductions. See *Financial Times*, November 4, 1990, p. 7, and Nigeria Supplement, March 12, 1991, p. III.

35 One popular means of attempting to avoid either expenditure cuts or tax rate increases is to annouce that "tax administration" will be improved, implying that tax revenues can be greatly increased simply by more effective enforcement of existing tax structures. While such measures are feasible, they usually take time to implement, and are not generally a means by which tax revenues can rapidly be increased.

making sufficiently large cuts has often been a major reason for failed policy reform efforts, as those cuts that are made at considerable political cost fall far short of the magnitude of what would be necessary to restore fiscal balance.

There are a number of ways that politicians who are not persuaded of the necessity for cuts of the necessary order of magnitude can *temporarily* affect the fiscal balance. Many of these techniques have little or possibly even a negative effect on longer-term fiscal balances. Postponing civil servants' salary increases, or even inflicting a salary cut of several months' duration, can reduce the short-term fiscal deficit yet will do nothing to alter the longer-term prospects. Equally, deferring maintenance of public infrastructure facilities, and/or temporarily reducing expenditures across the board or halting work on investment projects in progress can, in the short run, reduce the government fiscal deficit. In the longer term, either these expenditures must be resumed in which case nothing fundamental is altered, or there must be a process which selectively reviews investment projects and maintenance. Given that selectivity always invites resistance on the part of those "selected out," there is far more likely to be a sustainable shift in public expenditures if selectivity is achieved at the outset.

On the revenue side, imposing additional tariffs and taxes on imports can collect more revenue and is a short-run path of least resistance. Even with respect to the money supply, the Central Bank can affect domestic credit outstanding on Fridays, or on the last days of the month and quarter, in a variety of ways that have nothing to do with the longer-term pressures of excess demand in the economy.

For my purposes, there are two things to be noted about these sorts of policies. On one hand, they are mostly temporary palliatives, and avoid any more painful actions – such as laying off parastatal workers or other civil servants, closing down a money-losing parastatal enterprise, or weeding out public sector investment projects that do not promise high payoffs – that would increase the efficiency of public sector expenditures in the longer run. In a sense, they are little more than a "doctoring of the books." On the other hand, some of the measures that may have some longer-lasting effects – such as raising tariffs and severely reducing maintenance expenditures – are measures that will over the longer run reduce the efficiency of and the rate of return to public and private expenditures and investments.

It is thus normally possible for politicians perceiving the necessity for some actions (perhaps to satisfy international lenders, a point to which I return below) both to underestimate the necessary extent of the adjustment and to cut expenditures and/or raise revenues in ways which do not address the fundamental problems associated with the existing policy stance, and which, in the longer run, offer no prospect of altering the longer-term trends in the economy. Examination of the fiscal balance six months after an announced policy reform effort therefore seldom provides insight as to the nature of the expenditure reductions or revenue increases.

Moreover, in circumstances in which cuts must be effected in a very short period of time, it is seldom possible to achieve the goal selectively. The consequence is predictable: across-the-board cuts, often with heavy emphasis on deferring maintenance. Over time, pressures arise to resume investment projects and to restore preexisting real wages of government employees. Often, maintenance – perhaps the component of expenditures with the highest short-term (and possibly even the long-term) real rate of return – is the only category of expenditures to be permanently reduced. The inevitable consequences are twofold: (1) the stop–go cycle, discussed earlier, repeats after a period of time; and (2) the real rate of return on private investments falls further as the necessary transport, communication, and other infrastructure deteriorates.

Ceilings on money creation by themselves can do little unless accompanied by shifts in government expenditures and revenues. However, even when there are fiscal cuts, measures to contain monetary expansion are necessary. One such measure is increases in nominal interest rates in order to encourage domestic savings (in part by reducing domestic incentives for capital flight) and to reduce the excess demand for loans. Other financial reforms have often contributed importantly to the greater efficiency of resource allocation, especially of new investible funds.[36]

Even though credit rationing was not entirely abandoned, Korea shifted from nominal interest rates below the rate of inflation to positive real interest rates in the mid 1960s; the Turkish reforms of the early 1980s were accompanied by virtually complete financial liberalization over the next eight years after initial measures made controlled rates positive in real terms; in Ghana, interest rates were initially raised above the rate of inflation, but, when they were later liberalized, nominal interest rates actually fell;[37] and the Mexican reforms have also resulted in nominal interest rates above the rate of inflation.

On the fiscal side, a number of countries have succeeded in significantly reducing expenditures or increasing tax revenues on a sustained basis. In Turkey, the 1980 reforms were accompanied by major increases in the prices of goods produced by state-owned enterprises, with a consequent sizeable reduction in the fiscal deficit. Moreover, most SOEs were released from government regulation of their prices, allowing them to increase prices consistent with their costs

36 In many developing countries, financial liberalization has been accompanied by a sharp increase in nominal interest rates. If the prevailing rate of inflation is subtracted from that interest rate at points during the liberalization process, the resulting "real" interest rate can be very high, causing some to doubt the efficacy of total financial liberalization. Regardless of whether financial liberalization should be complete or not, however, all observers would agree that nominal interest rates below the rate of inflation are not consistent with efficient resource allocation. See Ronald I. McKinnon, *Financial Liberalization, Monetary Control, and Economic Development*, Johns Hopkins Press (Baltimore), 1991, for an analysis of the effects of financial repression and an in-depth analysis of financial liberalization episodes.

37 Abbey, *On Promoting Successful Adjustment.*

and market conditions. Simultaneously, they were no longer permitted to borrow (virtually automatically) from the Central Bank. Thus, there was a permanent shift of about 5 percent of GNP resulting from an altered mechanism for financing SOEs. Korean budgetary reforms in 1964 succeeded in imposing constraints on the government budget that virtually eliminated deficits thereafter.[38]

On the revenue side, a few countries have encountered dramatic success in raising revenue. This has been most notable in cases where informal markets had largely replaced official markets in the pre-reform situation. In Ghana, for example, government revenue constituted 19.6 percent of GNP in 1965, but had fallen to 5.5 percent of GNP by 1983. Thereafter, revenues rose, reaching 14.4 percent of GNP by 1987.[39] By 1989, it was estimated that the tax reform implemented as part of the overall policy package was responsible for having raised government revenues by 10 percentage points of GNP.[40]

In the Ghanaian case, additional revenues were sorely needed for immediate repair and rehabilitation of the ports, and other expenditures without which a supply response would have been very constrained. The more frequent situation, however, is when expenditure cuts must bear the brunt of the reduction. This is especially so when large subsidies and transfers have accounted for much of the fiscal deficit. The Egyptian experience, where wheat subsidies alone reached 12 percent of GNP, was detailed in the first lecture.

38 See David Cole and Princeton N. Lyman, *Korean Development, The Interplay of Politics and Economics*, Harvard University Press (Cambridge) 1971. Chile also successfully eliminated large budget deficits in the process of reform, changing the fiscal balance from a deficit equal to 9 percent of GNP in 1984 to a surplus of 3 percent of GDP in 1988. See Corbo and Solimano, "Chile's Experience with Stabilization, Revisited," p. 36.
39 Data from International Monetary Fund, *International Financial Statistics*, Yearbook, 1990, Ghana page.
40 Abbey, *On Promoting Successful Adjustment*, p. 10.

As with many other subsidy programs, the budgetary costs are large relative to the values received by the intended beneficiaries,[41] and targetted subsidy programs for the poor can achieve the intended purpose with a fraction of the cost of the preexisting plans.

On the macroeconomic front, the difficulties discussed thus far have been encountered by almost all countries whose governments have started stabilization programs. The political resistance to sufficiently large cuts is considerable, and the natural result is "too little, too late." The Brazilian experience with the cruzado plan illustrates how things can go wrong, and go wrong in major ways. The cruzado plan was a major adjustment plan announced by the Brazilian authorities in February 1986. Although it was seen as an "alternative" to an orthodox stabilization plan, it nonetheless was developed on the premise that the excess of government expenditures over receipts would be cut to zero, that that would halt inherent inflationary pressures, and that a price–wage freeze would halt "inertial inflation." For several months, the recorded rate of inflation was close to zero. Thereafter, inflation once again rose. By 1988–9, it averaged 20 percent per month, contrasted with an average of 11 percent per month in the two years preceding the start of the plan.[42] But, as Cardoso reports,

There is no controversy about the reasons why the Cruzado Plan failed. The most prominent factor was the overheating of the economy through loose fiscal and monetary policies, as well as through the overly generous wage policy. On the fiscal side, tax revenues disappointingly rose only a little, revenues

41 See Anne O. Krueger, *A Synthesis of the Political Economy in Developing Countries, The Political Economy of Agricultural Pricing Policy*, Volume 5 of Anne O. Krueger, Maurice Schiff, and Alberto Valdés (eds). Johns Hopkins University Press (Baltimore), forthcoming.
42 Eliana Cardoso, "From Inertia to Megainflation: Brazil in the 1980s," National Bureau of Economic Research Working Paper No. 3585, January 1991, table 2.

of state-owned companies were hurt by the price freeze, spending ran higher than anticipated, and subsidies that were cut during 1983–84 staged a comeback in 1986. The public sector wage bill also increased in line with the economy-wide trend [and] loose monetary policy produced very low interest rates that permitted firms lacking confidence in the program to build up speculative stocks.[43]

Trade and Payments Regime Reforms

If all that had to be done was to reduce the fiscal deficit and therefore presumably slow the growth of the money supply, the problem confronting policy makers in the crisis situation would be difficult enough. However, it is necessary also to consider the trade and payments regime aspects of the policy reform package. For changes in the trade and payments regime are crucial and also interact strongly with fiscal and monetary measures.

As noted earlier, probably the majority of policy reform programs have been inaugurated because of discomfort with the balance of payments/foreign exchange situation. Very often, foreign exchange reserves and lines of credit have been exhausted when the program is undertaken. In some instances, debt-servicing obligations are coming due and simply cannot be met. Capital flight may also be a significant contributing factor.

Usually, some adjustment in the nominal exchange rate is essential simply because the existing official rate has diverged so far from the black market rate that smuggling and other evasions of the trade and payments regime have become a major problem.[44] Export earnings have fallen, and those who

43 Cardoso, "From Inertia to Megainflation," pp. 11–12.
44 This had happened in Turkey by 1980 and in Ghana by 1983. In addition to concerns about the economic health of the nation, a major motive for policy on the part of government officials is often to regain the authority of the state over border transactions.

can keep their assets abroad do so. A devaluation of the currency in these circumstances can prompt an immediate reverse capital flow, as holders of assets abroad repatriate them under the new, more attractive, exchange rate.

However, when the motive of the policy reform program is to achieve a fundamental change in economic growth prospects, far more thoroughgoing reforms of the trade and payments regime are called for. If the regime is to be altered from a highly restrictionist, import-substitution oriented one to an outer-oriented, open economy, quantitative restrictions must be dismantled and tariff rates reduced.

For reasons already outlined, an exchange rate alteration is almost always a necessary component of a policy reform package. Not only is inflation likely to have outpaced nominal devaluations, but the authorities are very likely to have attempted to reduce the rate of inflation by suppressing the rate of exchange rate adjustment even when some exchange rate alterations were undertaken.

Moreover, if the changes in policies are genuinely designed to improve future growth prospects, as well as to handle the immediate crisis, the existing trade regime needs alteration, including a dismantling of quantitative restrictions on imports and a significant reduction in tariff rates and in the variation in tariff levels across commodity classes.[45]

If those changes are undertaken, incentives for export are improved in three ways: a more realistic exchange rate makes exporting inherently more attractive relative to production for the home market; the removal of protection to import-competing goods reduces the incentives that have been pulling resources into those activities; and access to the international

45 Note again the apparent conflict between revenue objectives associated with the desirability of reducing the fiscal deficit and the trade regimes objectives of inducing more resources into producing exportables.

market for intermediate inputs and raw materials cuts down the extent to which protection creates a high-cost environment for exporting firms.

Removal of quantitative restrictions and high tariffs is opposed by those businessmen, workers, and public sector employees engaged in production behind high walls of protection. And, while opposition to government expenditure cuts and tax increases can be strenuous, opposition to cuts in levels of protection can be even more so. If lobbyists and pressure groups are sufficiently politically powerful to resist or reverse some reductions in levels of protection, pressures from others threatened with deprotection mount and judgments about the viability of the reform program inevitably become more pessimistic.

If the shift in trade orientation is to succeed, it is vital that there are pulls of resources into exporting at the same time as there are pressures on import-competing industries to contract.[46] That, in turn, means that the required adjustment in the real exchange rate must be sufficient not only to offset past real appreciation (given the structure of protection) and any unsustainable component of the current account deficit, but also to increase the attractiveness of exports. With a freely flexible exchange rate, removal of tariffs or quantitative restrictions would be expected to result in currency depreciation; when there is a devaluation to a new fixed

46 In some instances, firms that held monopoly or quasi-monopoly positions in the domestic market and that were high-cost have been able to make sharp reductions in their cost structure once incentives have been changed. This can come about because of increased specialization within individual plants in fewer lines of output, because of rationalizations, or for other reasons. This phenomenon has been documented in Turkey, Anne O. Krueger and Baran Tuncer, "Growth of Factor Productivity in Turkish Manufacturing Industry," *Journal of Development Economics*, 11 (3), December 1982, pp. 307–25, and in Chile, Vittorio Corbo and Jaime de Melo, "Lessons from the Southern Cone Policy Reforms," *World Bank Research Observer*, 2(2), July 1987, pp. 111–42.

exchange rate, the magnitude of the necessary adjustment should be sufficient to increase the profitability of new entrants into exporting.

Clearly, in instances where policy reforms bring about major improvements in growth prospects, a significant sustained alteration in the real exchange rate is a key part of the policy reform package. This was certainly the case in Korea in the early 1960s, as the authorities used uniform, nondiscretionary export subsidies in addition to the official exchange rate to provide adequate incentives for exporting. In Turkey, the Turkish lira depreciated by more than the rate of inflation over the 1980–5 period as tariffs were removed and incentives for exporting increased as an offset.[47]

However, whether and in what quantities resources will flow into exportable activities depends not only on the magnitude of the initial policy changes, but also on judgments as to the likelihood that the new real exchange rate, and the realigned relative incentives provided by the trade and payments regime, will persist.

That assessment will depend on the type of exchange-rate regime chosen. If, as is sometimes the case, a new fixed exchange rate is announced, businessmen will then base their assessments regarding the sustainability of the real exchange rate on their evaluation of the fiscal-monetary package and therefore on the future expected rate of inflation. Unless inflation is expected to decelerate rapidly to a rate close to the world rate, it is unlikely that long-term production plans will be based on the real exchange rate implied initially by the nominal exchange rate selected. Further, even when there is an initial response to the altered real exchange rate, it

47 See Frank, Kim, and Westphal, *Foreign Trade Regimes and Economic Development*, table 5.9, p. 72 for estimates of the evolution of the real effective exchange rate for exports during the 1960s in Korea. For the 1980s in Turkey, see Anne O. Krueger and Okan Aktan, *Swimming Against the Tide: Turkish Trade and Economic Reforms in the 1980s*, Institute for Contemporary Studies (San Francisco), forthcoming.

cannot be sustained at a fixed nominal exchange rate in the face of strong inflationary pressures.[48] If a crawling peg regime is chosen, with the announcement that the nominal exchange rate will be altered to maintain the real exchange rate, the prospects for a rapid response by exporters to the altered regime are much more favorable.

But there is another major difficulty. For, while the objectives of the policy reform program include encouraging exportable production, they also include reducing the rate of inflation. In these circumstances, some advocate using the nominal exchange rate as an "anchor" for inflation control, and believe that permitting changes in the nominal exchange rate will make the reduction in the rate of inflation that much more difficult.[49]

This strategy is clearly tempting and had been used in more than a few instances.[50] In the 1960s and 1970s, the

48 See Tercan Baysan and Charles Blitzer, "Turkey," in Demetris Papageorgiou, Michael Michaely, and Armeane M. Choksi (eds), *Liberalizing Foreign Trade, New Zealand, Spain and Turkey*, Volume 6, Basil Blackwell (Cambridge, MA), 1991.

49 It is because of this set of considerations that some economists believe that trade policy reforms should not necessarily be a part of the initial policy package, but that liberalizing the trade and payments regime should wait until inflation is controlled. See, for example, Dani Rodrik, "Liberalization, Sustainability and the Design of Structural Adjustment Programs," mimeo, October 1988. See also Stanley Fischer, "Macroeconomics and Development," paper presented at the National Bureau of Economic Research Annual Conference on Macroeconomics, Cambridge, MA, March 1991.

50 For some countries undergoing policy reform, devaluation has had yet another effect which has increased the magnitude of the required fiscal adjustment. When the nominal price of foreign exchange is increased, as it must be in the face of a balance-of-payments-inflation crisis, not only do domestic nominal prices of exportables rise, but foreign debt-servicing obligations denominated in domestic currency increase, thereby increasing the magnitude of adjustment required in the government fiscal balance. This has

norm was for a discrete devaluation to a new, fixed nominal exchange rate, and the result was that, when macroeconomic adjustments had not been sufficient to control inflation, any alterations in the trade and payments regime were quickly reversed.[51] The famous "tablitas" of Argentina, Uruguay, and Chile in the late 1970s and early 1980s were efforts to bring down the domestic rate of inflation by "prefixing" the exchange rate, and hoping that domestic prices would converge.[52] They failed to do so, and instead a balance of payments crisis in each instance forced a large, discrete exchange rate change and spelled the end of any hope for the success of the overall program. Currently, Mexico has a prefix implicit in "El Pacto," and there is a gradual appreciation of the real exchange rate in consequence. At the time of writing, the Algerian authorities are reluctant to adjust the exchange rate by a realistic amount because of their concern about triggering inflation.[53]

However, failure to make an adequate adjustment in the exchange rate normally only postpones the date when a large, discrete devaluation, or a shift to a floating rate, must take place, either because an unrealistic exchange rate has resulted

---

provided another basis on which to oppose devaluations or to reduce their magnitude.

51 In fact, a major lesson that emerged from the National Bureau of Economic Research project on Foreign Trade Regimes and Economic Development was that a cardinal policy error was to tie the success of reforms in the trade and payments regime to that of inflation control. See Anne O. Krueger, *Foreign Trade Regimes and Economic Development, Liberalization Attempts and Consequences*, Ballinger Press (Lexington, MA), 1978.

52 See Vittorio Corbo and Jaime de Melo "Lessons from the Southern Cone Policy Reforms," pp. 111–42, for a description of the policies adopted in these countries, and an analysis of the failure of the three prefix programs.

53 *Financial Times*, January 28, 1991, Algeria Supplement, p. III. At that time, it was reported that the black market rate for the dinar was approximately one-fifth of the official exchange rate.

in another stop–go cycle, or because the hoped-for shift toward an outward orientation does not occur. Since observers recognize the pressures conducing to further exchange rate adjustment, whatever reduction does take place in the inflation rate may be regarded as transitory. Moreover, when all observers anticipate a further discrete exchange rate adjustment, the credibility of the entire reform program is called into question, responses to altered incentives are weaker, and the likelihood of success of the entire reform package is jeopardized.

An in-depth study sponsored by the World Bank of 18 countries' experience with trade liberalization led to the following conclusion:

> Experience shows a strong relationship between the *immediate* behavior of the real exchange rate, following the launching of liberalization, and the survivability of the experiment; the policy is likely to be sustained when the exchange rate increases, and to collapse when it falls. An increase of the real exchange rate appears to be almost a necessary condition for at least partial survival of a liberalization policy. The same relationship appears between the behavior of the real exchange rate *during* the life of the liberalization episode and its eventual fate. . .
>
> This relationship helps explain the positive association between the *strength* of a liberalization policy and its chance of being sustained: in most of the "strong" episodes, the real exchange rate *increased* following the launching of the liberalization policy . . .
>
> In achieving a *persistent* increase of the real exchange rate, a *substantial* initial nominal devaluation would make an important contribution. Contractionary fiscal or monetary policy appears to be important (though not so vital) for achieving a real devaluation.[54]

54 Michael Michaely, Demetris Papageorgiou, and Armeane M. Choksi, *Liberalizing Foreign Trade: Lessons of Experience in the Developing World*, Basil Blackwell (Cambridge, MA), 1991, pp. 196–7.

Other Policy Changes

There can be little question in theory or in practice that trade policy, exchange rate, fiscal, and monetary reforms must constitute the core of any reform program. To be sure, these short words cover a multitude of changes, as policies toward parastatals, subsidies and other transfers, public sector investment, and tax structures must be changed.

In individual situations, other initial policy changes are an essential part of the initial policy package. Raising the nominal rate of interest at least to the rate of inflation, and reducing the scope for misallocation of credit at an early stage of a reform effort has already been mentioned. But there are other bottlenecks that may require immediate dismantling: public monopolies over marketing and distribution may need to be broken; mechanisms for privatization may be introduced; roads or ports may be in need of immediate maintenance, and so on. Which of these measures is initially necessary and which can be postponed to a later point in a reform program is a matter of judgment, although some criteria and lessons are discussed in section 4.

Here, the point is that almost all of these steps are painful, politically and economically. Inevitably there will be cries of pain from interested parastatal managers and employees, urban workers whose food and energy prices were previously more heavily subsidized, and others who oppose the government or the reforms. Moreover, bureaucrats will resist changes if the changes may entail losing their power to allocate credit, import licences, and rationed food, or if their jobs are threatened by the closure of particular investment schemes or public sector enterprises. In some instances, these latter resistances can undermine the execution of a reform program even when there is reasonable consensus among the public at large and the politicians that reforms must be made.

The major lesson that arises from all these considerations is that it is far better to avoid getting into the difficulties that lead to the necessity for policy reforms! But that is a precept that should have been learned several decades ago: it is far easier to permit the accretion of government expenditures, institutions, and employees than it is to find means of improving the efficiency of the public sector and to reduce the imbalance in government budgets.

But, in practice, policies must be altered if growth prospects (and prospects for resumption of creditworthiness and new capital inflows) are to be improved. The difficulties are enormous: how to bring about governmental expenditure cuts in a sustainable way that will enhance, rather than impair, the productivity of infrastructure and other essential services; how to reconcile the anti-inflationary objectives with those pertaining to the trade regime; and how to identify those other policies within the economy which must be altered if the realigned incentives and policies are to be felt by decision makers within the economy.[55]

4 How Much Reform Should There Be and How Rapidly Should It Be Undertaken?

For policy makers intent upon policy reform, and for economists generally, there is little disagreement with what has been said thus far. For the most part, disagreement comes over three issues: (1) the necessary magnitude of reforms – how

55 There are usually myriad regulations and rules that govern price formation and resource allocation in the heavily regulated economies. Identification of those which can seriously impair the signals otherwise given by changed incentives is imperative, yet difficult. For example, price controls (or agricultural marketing boards) over export crops can effectively prevent any change in the exchange rate from affecting incentives for agricultural production for export; preferential treatment given to public sector enterprises' imports in congested ports can effectively prevent access to the international market by exporters for their needed inputs; and domestic content requirements or other measures may remain in place that reduce or even obviate the impact of tariff reductions.

much the exchange rate should be devalued, what the uniform tariff rate should be, by what percentage agricultural prices should be immediately increased, how much the nominal interest rate should be raised, how much public sector expenditures should be immediately cut and how much taxes raised, and so on;(2) the range of reforms to be undertaken initially; and (3) the speed at which reforms should be introduced.

These issues arise when the particulars of a reform program must be determined. It is not enough to say that the exchange rate should be altered, or that government expenditures should be cut: it is necessary to specify the magnitudes of those changes, and, in the case of government expenditures and tax revenues, to specify the precise means by which cuts will be carried out.

It is in confronting these questions that the difficulties already noted really come to the fore. For economic science is not yet at a point where the quantitative magnitudes of necessary reforms could be determined, *even if* the future prices of major exports, the behavior of the weather, and other important exogenous variables were known with certainty.[56] If one thinks of devising a reform program for a country whose terms of trade will improve 10 percent, whose harvest will be good, and where there will be large reverse capital flows following devaluation, it is clear that the order of magnitude of the required fiscal, monetary, and exchange rate adjustments will be smaller than if one or more of those three factors is less favorable.

Because cutting government expenditures, raising tax rev-

---

56 Some years ago, Richard Cooper examined the outcomes of a number of devaluation efforts. His statistical results suggested that one of the most important explanatory variables in explaining successful devaluations was the state of the weather (and thus the harvest) *after* devluation! Richard N. Cooper, "Devaluation in Developing Countries," in Gustav Ranis (ed.), *Government and Economic Development*, Yale University Press (New Haven), 1971. He also found that a surprisingly high fraction of finance ministers lost their jobs within 18 months of devaluation.

enues, altering the exchange rate, and reducing protection are all politically painful acts, it is natural for politicians to want do do as little as possible to achieve their goals. In circumstances of genuine uncertainty, not to mention the absence of knowledge about the precise elasticity of export response to an altered exchange rate and about the exact magnitude of other parameters, it is likely that programs actually put in place will be of smaller magnitude than are consistent with "safe" or assured favorable results. In practice, many of the programs that have been announced in the 1980s, and termed "policy reform packages" have been of the "too little, too late" variety, given the actual outcomes of exogenous events. In many of those cases, it is possible to imagine alternative scenarios (better terms of trade, better weather, etc.) under which the changes might have had more lasting effects, but it often would have required exceptional good fortune to witness such a favorable constellation of events. Ironically, the same politicians who blame their country's economic ill-fortunes on the adverse international environment simultaneously implicitly assume that that same environment will be highly favorable immediately after they institute their reforms!

I shall argue in the third lecture that increasing understanding of reform programs and of the responses to them can contribute to improved decision making, especially with regard to the necessary magnitude and margin of safety desirable in reform programs. Here, however, the other two questions must be addressed. These are the issues that are repeatedly raised in the literature, often in a manner designed to cast doubt upon the likelihood of successful reforms. Interestingly, the two are closely interrelated, although that linkage has not always been made clear.

In considering each of them, two issues are probably paramount: (1) the credibility of the reform program; and (2) the administrative capacity of the government. Reforms will have positive results more rapidly, the more people are convinced that reforms are irreversible. A major consideration in designing reform programs, therefore, is to achieve the maximum possible credibility.

Administrative capacity is an issue in most developing

countries, because the ranks of individuals with the necessary administrative and substantive competence are relatively thin. Stretching scarce personnel over too many issues at one time inevitably dilutes the extent to which even announced reforms are carried out, and it is probably wise (both for credibility reasons and for implementation) to defer secondary issues, and especially secondary issues which will require substantial administrative and technical resources, until later stages of the reform program.

These considerations of credibility and conserving scarce administrative and political resources are paramount when it comes to the "timing and sequencing" of reforms. Here, questions have been raised concerning the speed with which, e.g., tariffs should be reduced and quantitative restrictions removed, and about "which markets to liberalize first."

To a certain degree, the question as to which markets to liberalize first has already been addressed: attaining some degree of macroeconomic balance through reduction of fiscal deficits (and, where possible, attaining additional resources as I shall discuss in the next section), moving to a realistic exchange rate, and liberalizing the trade and payments regime are clearly necessary first steps. It is to some degree a matter of the circumstances of each individual country as to whether other essential first steps must be taken: removal of food subsidies, or raising the nominal rate of interest to reduce the subsidy component of lending, or reducing the deficit of parastatal enterprises can be crucial in given circumstances.

If there is consensus regarding priorities among markets, it probably centers around two propositions. First, freeing up prices and letting them more or less reflect border prices for traded goods and relative scarcities for factors of production and home goods is a necessary first step, and should be completed as soon as possible. This is both because a major objective of policy reform is to alter the allocation of resources and the efficiency with which they are used, and because, as stated earlier, if the exchange rate is not adjusted the credibility of any reduction in excess demand pressures will be questioned, while failure to make macroeconomic adjustments makes changes in the trade regime incredible.

The second item of consensus is related to the first: it is almost certainly unwise to contemplate a rapid liberalization of foreign exchange transactions in assets, and especially foreigners' access to existing domestic assets. Such a liberalization of capital account transactions should be deferred until *both* current account transactions in the balance of payments *and* the domestic financial market are liberalized. If capital account transactions are liberalized while protectionist barriers are still in place, asset prices normally would reflect expectations about future earnings streams. Until relative prices have been permitted to adjust to those that more or less reflect trade-offs between activities, it cannot be expected that the assets conveying the rights to future earnings streams would appropriately reflect the capitalized value of those streams. Conversely, if the financial market is not liberalized, capital outflows may take place in response to higher nominal yields abroad (or inflows may finance consumption expenditure).

In this regard, the experience of the Southern Cone countries, where capital inflows were induced by high domestic interest rates when the exchange rate was guaranteed to rise much more slowly, is instructive. A temporary domestic consumption and investment boom was financed by short-term capital inflows which reversed when the current account deficits grew in response to the appreciating real exchange rates.

There is a great deal to be said for creating favorable conditions for private foreign investment and encouraging foreigners' investment in new assets and earnings streams. It is far more questionable whether there should be liberalization of the entire capital account until there has been time for factors of production to respond to altered relative price signals.

Except for the capital account of the balance of payments, it is not obvious that there is any market in which reform should necessarily be delayed. In practice, there are a number of obstacles – laws to be changed, administrative procedures to be followed, parliamentary approvals to be gained, etc. – to speed of movement, and these in fact slow down reform programs quite enough.

There are several arguments for moving quickly, and they all center around the issue of the credibility and sustainability of reform. When relative prices and incentives for different activities are changed, the benefits of those changes will come only when economic agents within the economy respond to them. As already pointed out, how quickly agents will respond will depend in large part on their judgment as to the sustainability and durability of the altered economic policies.

For this reason, there is danger of a vicious circle: decisions to respond to altered incentives may be delayed because political opposition to the reforms raises questions as to their sustainability. Simultaneously, the fact that economic activity is not reviving in response to altered incentives provides grist for the mill of the opponents of change. To add to the magnitude of the problem, financial and other constraints may well result in fairly immediate hardship for those directly affected by the removal of quantitative restrictions, the closure of public sector enterprises, the price increases of previously subsidized energy, food, or transportation, or the shutting down of public investment projects.

One piece of evidence that observers may use to assess the likelihood that reforms will be sustained is the commitment of policy makers within the government to the reforms. That commitment, in turn, will be to a degree reflected in the magnitude of initial changes. If first steps are tentative, with announcement of a long-drawn-out schedule of tariff reductions, removal of subsidies, or other changes, observers may conclude that reforms are unlikely to succeed: rapidity and boldness may enhance credibility, and thus speed response, and then mitigate opposition to reforms.[57] The case has been put forth forcefully by Roger Douglas, the Finance Minister of New Zealand for the first several years of New Zealand's economic reforms, who gave the name "Rogernomics" to the entire program:

57 Dani Rodrik, "Liberalization, Sustainability and the Design of Structural Adjustment Programs," mimeo, October 1988, has forcefully made this point.

Even at maximum speed, the total [reform] program will take some years to implement, and the short-term tradeoff costs start from Day One . . .

There are serious dangers in seeking to hold down the pace of change . . . Policy cannot be fine-tuned with enough precision to ensure that, for example, inflation will be reduced successfully by a modest and targeted amount every year over an extended period. If an attempt is made to do so, it takes only a modest error or a miscalculation to move you backwards instead of forwards, thus destroying your credibility. . .

Vested interests seeking to preserve their privileges will always argue strongly for a slower pace of change. It gives them more time to mobilise public opinion against the reform. On the other hand, vested interests cannot obtain the pay-off from change until the government has moved far enough to reduce the costs imposed on them by the privileges of other interests. . .

It is uncertainty, not speed, that endangers the success of structural reform programs. Speed is an essential ingredient in keeping uncertainty down to the lowest achievable level . . . Before you can plan your perfect move in the perfect way at the perfect time, the situation has already changed. Instead of a perfect result, you wind up with a missed opportunity. . .

Some decisions take full effect the day they are made. Others take two to five years before they can be fully implemented. Perfect sequencing is just not achievable. If a window of opportunity opens up for a decision or action that makes sense in the medium term, use it before the window closes.[58]

The argument for speed rests ultimately on considerations of credibility, which in turn depends on the commitment of the government to the reform program. It will require actions

---

58 Roger Douglas , "The Politics of Successful Structural Reform," *Policy*, 6 (1), Autumn 1990. Some of Douglas's principles of "politically successful reform" are: (1) Implement reform in quantum leaps, using large packages; (2) Speed is essential: it is impossible to go too fast; (3) Once you start the momentum rolling, never let it stop; (4) Never sell the public short; (5) Don't blink: public confidence rests on your composure.

to make the commitment credible. However, there is no evidence that going more slowly "reduces pain": insofar as going slowly slows the speed of response, it is likely that the opposite is the case.

5 The Role of the International Institutions and Aid Agencies

One of the focal points for controversy over reform programs has been the role of the international institutions – primarily the International Monetary Fund, but also the World Bank, the regional development banks, and the foreign aid agencies in the major donor countries. The international institutions have often played key roles in policy reform programs. In some instances, officials of those agencies have been engaged in policy dialog with concerned individuals in the country in question. On occasion, their arguments and inputs have been identifiable as factors influencing national officials who, in turn, have sold the program within the government.[59]

More frequently, however, the major involvement of the international institutions and donors has come about because a balance-of-payments crisis precipitated the decision to change policies. In some cases, the national authorities have undertaken changes and later sought IMF standby and World Bank structural adjustment loans.[60] In many more instances,

59 There is considerable evidence that US aid officials in Korea were instrumental in persuading the Korean authorities that a change in economic policies would be desirable. Not only did aid officials themselves make the arguments, but many Korean nationals who later became instrumental in economic policy earlier worked in the US aid mission. See Cole and Lyman, *Korean Development*.

60 This was the case in Turkey in 1980, for example. See Osman Okyar, "Turkey and the IMF: A Review of Relations, 1978–82," in John Williamson (ed.), *IMF Conditionality*, Institute for International Economics (Washington, DC), 1983.

however, an IMF team has negotiated with the relevant officials in the country over terms on which a standby or extended fund facility will be granted.

Typically, when these negotiations are successful, they conclude with the signing of a "letter of intent," which is an official communication from the country to the Managing Director of the IMF and which sets forth quantitative targets for various key policy indicators – money supply, domestic credit, government expenditures, etc. – over the near-term future (often two years). These letters of intent are not public documents, and it is therefore difficult to assess their contents. In any event, one would have to have knowledge of the negotiations leading to them before a number of questions could be satisfactorily addressed.

As mentioned in section 1 of this lecture, in the 1980s, the World Bank has been integrally involved in reform programs, lending in structural adjustment loans (SALs) and sectoral adjustment loans (SECALs) to address key policy issues in particular sectors of the economy, such as energy, agriculture, and foreign trade, to support policy reforms addressing some of the underlying difficulties in the economy. Typically, however, the Bank has not supported reform programs with SALs unless IMF programs are already in place or the IMF indicates that conditions are such that they would be willing to consider a standby if so requested.

When the national authorities are in any event intent upon reform and seek primarily financial support from the IMF, the World Bank, and donor agencies, few problems arise. Problems, and criticisms of the international institutions, are greater: (1) when there is less domestic consensus as to the need for policy reform; (2) where the primary motive of major decision makers appears to be their desperation for foreign exchange to finance imports; and (3) when the short-run results of the program result in considerable economic hardship.

It is in those cases that "IMF conditionality" is attacked as an infringement on national sovereignty and as an arbitrary set of conditions imposed by international civil servants on helpless national authorities.[61] What is ignored is that the counterfactual – what would have happened in the absence of reform – is not known and the alternative might be worse yet. In many instances, reforms are started in crisis circumstances, as discussed earlier. Critics very often assume that things could have proceeded as they were, when in fact even the crisis situation was unsustainable!

Even then, the caricature of an "unwilling government" upon whom reforms are foisted is overly simplistic. In almost all circumstances, there are those in government who advocate changes in policy and those who oppose them. Clearly, the international institutions can strengthen the hands of those in government advocating economic policy reforms, both by providing technical support and by refusing, as they should, to support programs that are reasonably certain to fail.

In some instances, politicians may even "hide behind the cloak" of the international agencies, using them as scapegoats for the necessary measures when indeed they support them. In other instances, when political pressures mount and/or economic difficulties generate resistance to reforms, opposing politicians may blame the international institutions for their difficulties.

It is certainly true that the IMF and the World Bank should not lend support to programs unless they are assured that the country's future economic performance will improve. It would make no sense for the IMF or the World Bank to lend – at interest rates near market terms – to countries whose response would be to persist in their excess spending until the funds are exhausted and the next balance-of-payments crisis emerges! Indeed, one can argue that in instances such as that of Argentina, where funds were disbursed in support of the first austral plan, that the Argentines are worse off: their inflation and the underlying fiscal and monetary

61 See John Williamson, *IMF Conditionality*, Institute for International Economics, (Washington, DC), 1983, for a collection of papers on this issue. See also Guitian, "Fund Conditionality".

excesses that resulted in it has persisted longer, and with that economic deterioration has been greater. Moreover, if and when Argentina does manage to adopt economic policies that reverse the decline, the outstanding burden of indebtedness will be greater than it would have been had the IMF and World Bank imposed even stricter conditions as a prerequisite for the loans.

There may, however, be a case to be made for efforts on the part of policy makers to inform the body politic as to their policy changes and why they are necessary. While, as noted earlier, greater public information and discussion prior to announcing reforms is not always feasible (as, for example, when gross foreign exchange reserves are exhausted and a change in the exchange rate must be made), opposition can in some cases be muted by greater discussion of the problems of the existing situation. Gaining widespread acceptance of reforms, however, seems best accomplished by their success. As such, the critical factor is the design of a credible and sustainable reform package.

As understanding of the reasons why poor policy leads to low growth and of the determinants of the likelihood of successful policy reform increases, the components of sustainable reform packages should be more widely accepted. The Bank and Fund will then be able to support reform programs with greater assurance that they represent sufficient changes to reverse the economic fortunes of the country concerned. Much of the resistance to reforms has come from fear of the effects of policy changes, which in turn has been fuelled by the very high number of programs inaugurated with great fanfare as "major reform programs" and which have, in many cases predictably, failed. Already, the experience of the two agencies, and the interaction of their staff with domestic policy makers, provides an important input of knowledge and comparative experience on which to base the formulation of reform programs. Especially in light of the crisis atmospheres in which many such programs are formulated, the availability of staff from international agencies with experience (both positive and negative) from other countries can provide an important resource additional to the financial resources that can support the program.

6 International Indebtedness and the Availability of Resources

At the outset of the first lecture, I mentioned the worldwide debt crisis of the early 1980s, and how the symptom of debt crisis became confused with the cause – weak underlying economic policies in the heavily indebted countries.

Having said that debt was not the major cause of underlying difficulties and that policy reform is essential, however, is not to deny the role of resources in permitting rapid response to reform efforts, and thereby increasing the economic returns in the initial period after reforms are instituted. That, in turn, is an important factor in reducing political opposition to reform programs during the period when resources are being reallocated to their newly profitable uses.

In principle, there *can* be a debt overhang: debt servicing obligations (on debt that was incurred without the offsetting investment in activities yielding high enough returns for its service) can be sufficiently large so that new investments don't pay. This could come about if the tax on new earnings streams necessary to finance the debt-service would make the after-tax returns sufficiently low so as to render investment unattractive. Jeffrey Sachs[62] has been perhaps the foremost proponent of the view that this is in fact the case in many developing countries, and that some form of debt relief is essential if growth is to resume.

It is difficult to see why there is an argument for debt

62 Jeffrey Sachs, "Introduction," in Jeffrey Sachs (ed.), *Developing Country Debt and Economic Performance*, University of Chicago Press, (Chicago), 1989.

relief, rather than new money, in instances where policy conditionality is necessary in order for reforms to succeed.[63] However, one can take the argument a step further. When policy reforms are sufficiently far-reaching to hold out promise of success, additional resources in support of those programs can reduce the necessary dislocations during the period of transition, and can permit the same transition with less economic dislocation in the interim.

Even without a debt overhang, however, additional resources can permit a less painful transition period as resources are reallocated. This is especially true when imports of intermediate goods and raw materials have been greatly compressed during the crisis preceding the reforms: additional foreign exchange can finance the resumption of import flows and thus permit the revival of economic activity. In a few cases, these flows have even permitted the increased use of capacity so that economic activity increased, rather than declined, as inflationary pressures were reduced and the economy stabilized.[64]

63 If debt relief requires resources (from aid agencies or international institutions) that could otherwise be used for new lending, there are several other questions that arise. If the resources entailed in new lending can be used to finance additional investments, whereas debt relief simply goes to permitting the government to resume voluntary debt-service, it would follow that the resources in question would have higher productivity in new lending. Moreover, it must be noted that if debt relief were aimed at the heavily indebted countries and did require the diversion of aid resources, the implicit redistribution would be from low-income countries (including notably the South Asian subcontinent), which did not borrow excessively, to middle-income countries, which did.

64 See Anne O. Krueger, _Foreign Exchange Regimes and Economic Development: Turkey_, Columbia University Press (New York), 1974, chapter 3, for an analysis of the Turkish devaluation of 1958, in which inflation was brought quickly under control and output expanded in response to the liberalization of imports which accompanied the stabilization package. See also Behrman, _Foreign Trade Regimes and Economic Development: Chile._ Behrman found devalu-

In addition, in some cases the availability of support for a reform program permits greater investment during the period of transition (possibly including highly desirable maintenance of infrastructure), and thus can mitigate the required reductions (but not reallocations) in former activities. It is arguable, for example, that the Bolivian reforms could by now have resulted in significantly more growth had additional resources been available from the international community, given the reduction in export earnings and the necessary domestic realignments. More generally, when policies are realigned to provide greatly increased incentives for exporting, expansion of exportable industries (and the infrastructure to support them) should be highly profitable. If capital inflows permit additional investment in the post-reform period, economic growth can accelerate more than in circumstances in which domestic investment must be financed entirely by domestic savings.

To be sure, when policy reforms must in any event be undertaken, there are always risks that additional resources will reduce the sense of urgency and thus diminish the magnitude of the changes made. Nonetheless, it is certainly arguable that if the international community had been somewhat less willing to lend token support to half-hearted and partial reform efforts, while simultaneously providing greater support for the more far-reaching and fundamental reforms, successes would have been greater, and some of the politically contentious discussions of IMF conditionality might have been reduced. Certainly, the record of support for failed programs is an argument in the hands of those opposing undertaking the dislocations inevitably entailed in policy reforms.

Had resources to support far-reaching reform programs been greater in the 1980s, successes would have come more rapidly and with smaller costs of dislocation. Conceivably

---

ation to be contractionary and inflationary, while liberalization of imports (which is possible only with financing) was expansionary and helped mitigate inflationary pressures.

policy makers in some other countries might then have been more favorably disposed to policy reform programs, thus perhaps further improving the prospects for adoption of sufficiently far-reaching reforms to improve growth prospects significantly.

In the next lecture, attention turns to experience with reforms, including both the economics and the politics of successful and unsuccessful reform programs.

3

Lecture Three
Experience with Reform Programs

In the first lecture, I argued that differences in developing countries' growth rates reflect, to a large degree, differences in the extent to which their economic policies are conducive to rapid economic growth. I also provided some indicators of the extent to which policies in some developing countries were highly inefficient and inconsistent with sustained rapid economic development. Then, in the second lecture, I focussed on the components of policy reform programs – what is involved, and what must be done. There were allusions to some of the difficulties that can be encountered with these programs, but little was said about what can be accomplished, or about actual experience with reforms.

In this last lecture, focus will be primarily on two issues. The first is on experience with reform programs, primarily with successful ones. The second is on what is coming to be called "the political economy of reform," which really addresses the question of how policy stances so inimical to growth can arise and be perpetuated. A concluding section turns to the issues of the need for research into a great many aspects of policies and their effects.

1 Successful and Unsuccessful Reforms

It would be ideal if economic knowledge had progressed far enough to have a general model of the interaction of economic policy with other factors affecting economic growth, and if one could then simply plug in the relevant parameters to the model to provide estimates of the changes in economic performance that can accompany a successful reform program. Because economies are complex and our understanding is as yet limited, however, efforts to understand what reform programs can accomplish must be more modest. And, because each country's policy stance prior to reforms, its endowment of factors of production, and its circumstances *vis-à-vis* the world economy are different, each program must be separately assessed.

Policy reform programs are therefore complex, and it seems preferable to discuss a few in some detail rather than to survey the quantifiable aspects of many.[1] The most spectacular growth performances of the past quarter century have been those of Taiwan and South Korea; both of those countries fundamentally reversed earlier economic policies before the mid 1960s. In part because it is now often forgotten just how poor those countries were and how their policies were similar to those of the poorly performing countries today, I shall start with a brief overview of Korean economic reforms and their aftermath. Since the Korean reforms began a long time ago, however, many observers object that that experience is not relevant to the 1980s. For that reason, I shall thereafter turn attention to Turkey, and the Turkish change in economic policies that began in 1980.

1 A good overview and analysis of aggregate experience in the 1980s is provided by Vittorio Corbo and Stanley Fischer, "Adjustment Programs and Bank Support: Rationale and Main Results," World Bank Country Economics Department, Working Paper No. 582, January 1991.

There are a number of other countries where reforms are underway that are either judged successful, or as showing considerable promise of success. Most notable among them are perhaps Chile, where economic growth has accelerated remarkably in the latter half of the 1980s after thoroughgoing policy reforms, and Thailand, where a more gradual policy reform program (from an initially less distorted policy stance) was followed by double-digit growth in the latter half of the 1980s. In addition, however, Ghana has experienced more than half a decade of growth averaging over 5 percent annually after that country's long economic deterioration of the preceding twenty years,[2] Mexico has undertaken major reforms in her trade and payments regime and a number of other sectors of the economy and growth is beginning to accelerate;[3] and Mauritius has averaged 7 percent annual average growth since 1983 and now is ranked as a middle-income country.[4] Many other countries' governments have undertaken policy reforms with the support of the World Bank and the IMF (see table 2.1 in Lecture Two), but it is too early to assess results.

Confining discussion to success stories would be misleading, however. I shall, therefore, conclude the discussion of experience with reforms on a pessimistic note, discussing Argentine economic policy reforms of the past decade. Again, other countries might equally be mentioned: Egypt, Zambia, Brazil, Sudan, Senegal, and many others have periodically

2 See Joseph L. S. Abbey, *On Promoting Successful Adjustment: Some Lessons from Ghana*, The 1989 Per Jacobsson Lecture, Per Jacobsson Foundation (Washington, DC), September 24, 1989.

3 Mexico's growth rate in 1990 is estimated to have been 3.9 percent, which is still low by historical standards. See *Financial Times*, Feb. 27, 1991, p. 8. This is not to say that Mexican success is assured. There are significant concerns that the exchange rate is being adjusted by less than the proportionate inflation differential. Should this continue, the reforms will become incredible and policy measures will have eventually to be taken.

4 *New York Times*, September 10, 1990, p. C6.

announced reforms of more or less sweeping scope and magnitude, only to have them fail when inflation reaccelerated, food riots led to the reinstitution of subsidies, the foreign exchange auction was abandoned, or other clear-cut indicators of the program's failure appeared.[5]

Korea

Korean economic growth has been so spectacular that it is now often forgotten just how poor Korea was, and how bleak that country's development prospects were judged to be. Korea was a Japanese colony from 1910 to the end of the Second World War. Korean reconstruction after the war had hardly more than begun (and the country was still administered by US military forces) when the peninsula was partitioned, giving the North most of the entire country's electric

5 There are also a large number of countries for whom reforms may be judged to have been partially successful. Bolivia is perhaps the most notable: the rate of inflation fell rapidly from 40,000 percent annually to very low levels, and fiscal reforms were fairly sweeping. However, although Bolivian reforms were successful in that dimension, economic growth has not accelerated. See Juan Antonio Morales and Jeffrey Sachs, "Bolivia's Economic Crisis," National Bureau of Economic Research Working Paper No. 2620. June 1988. The Sri Lankan reforms after 1977 might be similarly judged: many government controls over private economic activity were eliminated, and growth accelerated, but a sharp increase in government spending resulted in increased macroeconomic instability. See Andrew G. Cuthbertson and Premachandra Athukorala, "Sri Lanka," in Demetris Papageorgiou, Michael Michaely, and Armeane M. Choksi, *Liberalizing Foreign Trade*, Vol. 5, Basil Blackwell (Cambridge, MA), 1991, pp. 333ff. Finally, mention should be made of the New Zealand policy reforms of the 1980s. See David Caygill, *Economic Restructuring in New Zealand since 1984*, The 1989 Per Jacobsson Lecture, Per Jacobsson Foundation (Washington, DC), September 24, 1989, and Anthony Rayner and Ralph Lattimore, "New Zealand," in Papageorgiou, Michaely, and Choksi, Vol. 6, 1991, pp. 1–136.

power generating capacity and industry. As adjustment to that shock started, the South was confronted with rapid inflation, multiple exchange rates, and other policies of the sort described in the first lecture. The American military command succeeded in starting several important changes, including educational reforms, land distribution (which was essential since most of the land had been owned by the Japanese), distribution of ownership claims to factories and other assets (which again had been in Japanese hands), and improvements in the distribution of agricultural inputs. Authority was also transferred from the American military to the Republic of Korea at the end of the 1940s.

Although economic activity grew rapidly, it had not yet reattained prewar levels by the time the Korean war started in 1950. Over the next three years, opposing armies moved up and down the Korean peninsula with attendant destruction several times before active hostilities ceased in the summer of 1953.

There then ensued a five-year period during which Korean economic policy displayed most of the excesses I described earlier. The government incurred sizeable fiscal deficits, considerably greater in size than the foreign aid received from the United States, itself equal to almost 10 percent of GNP. The domestic savings rate was negative, with total investment financed by the inflation tax or by foreign aid. The resulting inflation rate was in excess of 20 percent annually – very high by the standards of the 1950s.

Exports constituted around 3 percent of GNP, and showed no systematic tendency to grow in the 1950s, as a multiple exchange rate system left the exchange rate chronically overvalued.[6] Quantitative restrictions on imports were used to

6 This was in part deliberate. President Sygmun Rhee believed that American aid would be larger, the larger was the apparent Korean deficit. He therefore purposely rejected policy measures that might have induced more exports. See David Cole and Princeton N. Lyman, *Korean Development, the Interplay of Politics and Economics*, Harvard University Press (Cambridge), 1971, pp. 170ff.

contain excess demand, despite periodic devaluations and alterations in the exchange rate system. Corruption surrounding the allocation of import licenses became a major political issue in the late 1950s.

Although a postwar recovery period offers unusual opportunities for rapid growth,[7] the annual average real rate of growth of Korean GNP remained around 5 percent in the 1953–7 period, and declined thereafter. Within the United States, a political debate ensued about whether South Korea was viable under any circumstances. It was taken for granted that South Korea could not grow: incomes were incredibly low, the density of population on arable land was then the highest in the world, and the low savings and export ratios led observers to believe that the best that could be hoped was to continue foreign aid to maintain living standards.[8]

After an extensive congressional debate, the American government announced that it would cut back its levels of foreign aid. In 1958, Korea embarked upon a stabilization program, the objective of which was to reduce excess demand for foreign exchange and to cut the domestic rate of inflation. This program was successful in the short run in reducing the domestic rate of inflation, but did little to address underlying structural issues. The Korean economy's performance in 1959 was even more sluggish than it had been in earlier years.

By that time, the level of corruption surrounding the allocation of import licenses was so great that it was not only public knowledge, but was repeatedly reported in the popular press. Disaffection with the Rhee regime's inability to deliver economic growth, and its increasingly chaotic controls, was increasing.

In addition, in response to the American decision to cut

7 These opportunities arise in part because investments can be allocated to projects where repairs, or replacement of damaged segments, can greatly increase capacity and capacity utilization.
8 See Anne O. Krueger, *The Foreign Sector and Aid*, Harvard University Press (Cambridge, MA), 1982, chapter 1, ff. 18.

back on foreign aid (which was the only source of net investment for the economy, as domestic saving was so small), there
followed a debate within South Korea about future prospects.
It was evident to all Koreans that, given the likely decline in
foreign aid, a country as natural-resource poor as South Korea
could anticipate future growth only if exports began growing.
At the same time, political disaffection with Sygman Rhee led
to a "student revolution" in 1960, and an overthrow of the
Rhee regime.

The new government was weak, for a variety of reasons,
and was replaced with a military government within a year.
Later still, elections were held under a new constitution, and
President Park Chun Hee came to office. Even under the
initial post-revolutionary government, however, some changes
in economic policy were made. A set of export incentives
applicable on a nondiscretionary basis to all exports of nontraditional goods[9] was instituted, and there was a significant
devaluation of the exchange rate. Thereafter, export incentives
were altered frequently, so that their value to exporters was
maintained relatively constant in real terms. In addition,
exporters were accorded the right to import needed intermediate goods, raw materials, and capital goods automatically and
duty free. Moreover, only exporters were permitted to import,
so that whatever value there was to import licenses was earned
through exporting. In addition, exporters were given access
to low-interest loans and rebates on some taxes.

The Park government continued these policies and moved
still further. Inflation had fallen fairly sharply after the stabilization of 1958, but began rising again after a failed harvest
in 1963. The authorities continued to adjust export subsidies
so as to maintain the real exchange rate for exports. Also, by

9 Korea's exports equalled, as already stated, only 3 percent of GNP
in 1960. 88 percent of those exports were primary commodities.

1963, quantitative restrictions on imports generally had been greatly reduced, and exporters continued to be the ones entitled to import.[10]

The response to the initial reforms was substantially greater than had been anticipated. As the data in table 3.1 indicate, exports, which had been only $30 million in 1960, reached over $100 million in 1964, and GNP growth began accelerating as well. In 1964, a second round of reforms was undertaken. Fiscal reforms were introduced, to restrict government expenditures to a level close to revenues. Subsequently, fiscal deficits were close to balance, as tax revenues rose both because of economic growth and because of improved tax collection. Interest rates were increased to positive real levels, and they have seldom since been so low as to give borrowers negative real interest rates.[11] In 1967, the Korean authorities altered the import licensing system still further: imports had previously been forbidden unless they were on a "positive" list of eligible imports. After the reform, imports were permitted unless they were expressly

10 The alteration in Korean policies therefore took place over the period from 1957–8 to 1964. Depending on the criteria employed, one could say that the reform period encompassed the entire seven-year period, that it took place in 1960 (the year when export incentives were strongly increased and the exchange rate moved to a more realistic level) or in 1964 when fiscal and monetary changes accompanied still further changes in the trade regime. If one examines outcomes, rather than policies, the strong growth of Korean exports began after 1960. These difficulties with precise dating of reform programs are not unique to Korea, and are fairly typical. They are one of the factors making cross-country comparisons of reforms difficult.

11 However, further financial liberalization proceeded only slowly until the 1980s. Credit rationing was still a major factor in resource allocation throughout the 1960s and 1970s, and exporters had first call upon available credit. See Charles R. Frank, Kwang Suk Kim, and Larry E. Westphal, *Foreign Trade Regimes and Economic Development: Korea*, Columbia University Press (New York), 1975.

Table 3.1. Korea's Economic Policies and Performance, 1955 to 1970

Year	Fiscal Deficit (% GNP)	Real Exchange Rate (1960 = 100)	Rate of Inflation (%)	Current Account (% GNP)	Export Earnings ($ million)	Growth of Real GNP (1970 prices)
1955	−3.2	76.9	68.2	−0.4	18	5.4
1956	−5.9	61.9	22.5	−0.4	25	0.4
1957	−4.5	55.1	23.1	0.0	19	7.6
1958	−0.5	57.8	−3.7	1.0	17	5.2
1959	−0.5	55.8	3.1	0.4	20	3.8
1960	1.0	63.6	10.2	0.3	33	2.0
1961	−0.1	115.9	8.3	1.4	41	4.8
1962	−2.8	114.0	6.7	−2.0	54	3.1
1963	0.0	94.7	19.7	−3.7	87	8.8
1964	0.2	120.4	29.5	−0.8	120	8.6
1965	0.1	135.5	13.6	0.3	175	6.1
1966	−0.6	126.2	12.3	−2.7	250	12.4
1967	−0.6	114.5	10.6	−4.1	335	7.8
1968	0.4	108.0	10.9	−7.4	486	12.6
1969	−2.0	104.1	12.5	−7.3	658	15.0
1970	−0.8	100.0	16.1	−7.1	835	7.9

Source: Charles R. Frank, Kwang Suk Kim, and Larry Westphal, *Foreign Trade Regimes and Economic Development: Korea,* Columbia University Press (New York), 1975, table 2.7 (for GNP growth rates); International Monetary Fund, *International Financial Statistics, Yearbook* (Washington, DC), 1990.

forbidden and on a "negative list." Over the next decade, the negative list grew gradually smaller and tariffs were also somewhat reduced.

Gradually, also, special export incentives – which were, it should be noted, uniform and nondiscretionary across all categories of exportable commodities – were gradually reduced, and the exchange rate was adjusted more frequently to maintain incentives fairly constant in real terms for exporters. In the first few years after the reform program began, it may fairly be said that the incentives for exportable and import-competing production were moved closer together in large part by the provision of export incentives, which offset part or all of the incentives provided by protection to import-competing industries. Thereafter, however, the relative importance both of tariffs and of export incentives was reduced, and the exchange rate came increasingly to be the mechanism for providing incentives to exportable and import-competing producers. By the mid 1980s, all special incentives for export conveyed through the tax system had been abolished, and there was little special incentive for exports remaining, other than through the exchange rate itself. Exchange rate unification was largely complete, although there remained tariffs on a number of imports of commodities for domestic consumption.

Reforms in other Korean markets followed similar patterns. Financial liberalization continued. After 1964, the Korean government's fiscal deficits were far smaller, although inflation remained a problem until the mid 1980s; after 1983, there followed five years in which the annual rate of consumer price increase was less than 1 percent.

One other aspect of Korean policies should be mentioned. Throughout the three decades of successful reform and growth, governmental policy was highly sensitive to the needs for good infrastructure in transport, communications, education, social services, and public health. In the 1950s, the focus of governmental attentions had been on the allocation of credit and import licenses; after the reforms, the primary focus of government economic policies was on assuring that ports, roads, telephones, mail, and other infrastructure would be adequate so as not to frustrate exporters' efforts to meet delivery dates on orders.

Table 3.1 gives some quantitative indicators of the changes in policy and the changes in economic performance. The overall results are too well known to require much comment here. Korea averaged over 10 percent real growth of GDP in the decade after 1963, with export growth a leading sector, averaging more than 40 percent annually. The Korean savings rate went from less than 3 percent of GNP in the late 1950s to 15 per cent in 1970 to about 35 percent by the mid 1980s – rising so much so that by 1986 the American government began pressuring Koreans to find ways to reduce their savings rate! Moreover, aid was phased out, but investment in Korea was so profitable that borrowing from commercial banks permitted a rate of investment substantially above the rate of savings throughout the 1970s and early 1980s. By the mid 1980s, the Korean savings rate had risen so much that Korea's current account swung into surplus, and some of the debt incurred earlier was repaid.

After about four years in the early 1960s during which nonagricultural employment expanded rapidly but real wages fell, nonagricultural employment expanded rapidly but real wages began rising at an average annual rate of 8 percent, and nonagricultural employment has risen rapidly enough so that unemployment has not been a problem for over a decade. In the 1950s, more than 60 percent of the population was engaged in agriculture; by the late 1980s, the proportion had fallen to less than 20 percent.

Export growth was the most spectacular sign of Korean success. Exports grew from 3 percent of GNP in 1960 to 46 percent of GNP by 1988, reaching 59 billion dollars in that year. Imports, of course, rose almost commensurately, as the change from import-substitution in the 1950s resulted in a structural change in the economy. Korean per capita income was estimated in 1987 to be $2,690, having increased in real terms at an average annual rate of 6.4 percent since 1965.

This transformed Korea from one of the poorest countries in Asia (arguably having a higher living standard than those on the Indian subcontinent) to one of the richest.[12]

Thus, from a very poor aid recipient with bleak growth prospects in the 1950s, South Korea was transformed by the late 1980s into a country whose exports were regarded by the United States as a "competitive threat." Indeed, South Korea's success was so complete that most observers now believe the South Korean case irrelevant for other developing countries! It should be noted that, despite the far-reaching nature of the alteration in the incentive structure and macroeconomic environment in the early 1960s, continued improvements in the policy stance in Korea have been a hallmark of continued growth. Except for Korean agriculture (which was strongly discriminated against until the 1970s, but which is now heavily protected), the policy changes have been uniformly toward providing incentives for the private sector that appropriately reflect the trade-offs confronting the Korean economy. In that sense, policy reform has been a continuing process. But from its outset, Korean policy makers were clear in their commitment to providing an environment in which exporters could, if they were able to produce efficiently, profit.

Turkey

If one examines the situation in countries where policy reforms are more recent, the results are naturally less dramatic. There was no point along the way at which Korean future successes were assured, and there is certainly no way to judge the long-term results of a change in policy that has

12 The Philippines, Thailand, Malaysia, and Burma were all estimated to have considerably higher living standards than Korea in the 1950s and 1960s; all are estimated to have much lower living standards today.

been in effect only over a period of several years. Nonetheless, it is worth examining the Turkish change in policies in the early 1980s.

Turkey was, historically, a much richer country than Korea. Tables 3.2 to 3.4 give some comparative data on the two countries as they pursued their divergent development paths from 1955 to 1980. As of the mid 1950s, the two countries had about the same population, but Turkish real GNP and per capita income was estimated to be about twice that of Korea. The two countries had similar economic structures, with 44.8 per cent of South Korea's GNP originating in agriculture, compared to 40.6 percent for Turkey in 1960, the first year for which comparable Turkish estimates are available. Turkish exports were much larger than Korea's however, at $313 million in 1955 compared to Korea's $17.6 million.

Turkish economic policies had been set in the 1930s: growth was to be led by import-substituting industrialization, with state-owned enterprises playing a leading role. In the 1950s domestic inflation began when there were large increases in government spending on infrastructure without offsetting increases in tax revenue. As domestic inflation accelerated, the prices at which SOEs sold their outputs were controlled in an effort to reduce the rate of inflation. The result, however, was increasing deficits of SOEs, which in turn were automatically financed by Central Bank credits.

During this inflationary period, the nominal exchange rate was held constant at the level that had been set in 1946. By the mid 1950s, excess demand for foreign exchange was mounting, and the black market premium for dollars was over 300 percent and was increasing rapidly. The Turkish authorities responded by imposing across-the-board import licensing in 1954 (restricting each importer to 95 percent the value of imports of 1953). Export earnings, however, were falling as the real appreciation of the Turkish lira (LT) made exporting less attractive and the buoyant domestic economy diverted goods to the domestic market. With foreign exchange reserves exhausted, the Turkish authorities tightened the

Table 3.2. Contrasts between Turkey and Korea, 1955 to 1985: Relative Living Standards

| | Turkey | | | Korea | | |
Year	Population (million)	Real GNP ($ million)	GNP/Capita ($ 1980)	Population (million)	Real GNP ($ million)	GNP/Capita ($ 1980)
1955	23.8	26,942	1,132	21.4	14,338	670
1960	27.5	34,513	1,255	25.0	17,250	690
1965	31.1	43,758	1,407	28.7	22,874	797
1970	35.3	60,081	1,702	32.2	38,286	1,189
1975	40.0	90,000	2,250	35.3	64,564	1,829
1980	44.4	102,964	2,319	38.1	90,259	2,369
1985	50.0	126,650	2,533	41.0	125,296	3,056

Source: Robert Summers and Alan Heston, "A New Set of International Comparisons of Real Product and Price Levels Estimates for 130 Countries, 1950–1985," *Review of Income and Wealth*, Series 34, No. 1, March 1988.

Table 3.3. Contrasts between Turkey and Korea, 1955 to 1985: Sectoral Structure, Share of GNP (at 1980 prices)

	Turkey				Korea			
		Industry					Industry	
Year	Agriculture	Total	(Mfg)	Services	Agriculture	Total	(Mfg)	Services
1955	n.a.	n.a.	n.a.	n.a.	49.4	8.9	(6.2)	41.7
1960	40.6	19.8	(11.4)	39.6	44.8	12.3	(8.5)	42.9
1965	34.4	24.0	(15.0)	41.6	41.3	16.3	(11.1)	42.4
1970	27.2	30.0	(21.8)	42.8	30.4	26.0	(15.6)	43.6
1975	23.3	30.4	(23.0)	46.3	24.7	32.7	(22.8)	42.6
1980	22.6	30.2	(21.1)	47.2	14.9	41.3	(29.7)	43.7
1985	20.4	32.3	(24.7)	47.3	13.4	45.6	(33.5)	41.0

n.a. Not available.
Source: World Bank, World Tables, 1984, 1989–90.

Table 3.4. Contrasts between Turkey and Korea, 1955 to 1985: Memorandum Statistics

	Turkey		Korea	
Year	Real Investment to GNP (%)	Export Earnings ($ million)	Real Investment to GNP (%)	Export Earnings ($ million)
1955	13.9	313	8.1	18
1960	16.3	321	6.7	33
1965	16.2	464	10.4	175
1970	22.0	588	23.5	835
1975	25.4	1,401	25.6	5,081
1980	21.7	2,910	28.9	17,505
1985	21.6	4,703	30.7	30,283

Sources: Real investment share: Summers and Heston, "A New Set of International Comparisons"; export: IMF, *International Financial Statistics Yearbook*, 1990.

import licensing regime. Finally, by 1957, there was no free foreign exchange, delays in issuing licenses extended over a year, and Turkish importers were no longer eligible even for suppliers' credits because of existing arrears in payments.

Like Korea, Turkey finally undertook a stabilization program in 1958. There was a once-and-for-all devaluation of the lira (from LT2.8 per US dollar to LT9 per dollar), a rationalization of the import licensing regime, and an agreement with the IMF which involved ceilings on credit and government expenditures, increases in prices of outputs of SOEs, and other measures.[13]

The short-run results of the stabilization program were very favorable. The rate of inflation fell from over 25 percent annually to 5 percent. Export earnings, which had been declining, rose rapidly, and real GNP increased 5 percent in 1959. Thereafter, Turkey grew reasonably rapidly by international standards in the 1960s, averaging about 6 percent annually, although foreign exchange difficulties reemerged in the late 1960s (as the real exchange rate had once again appreciated and import licensing delays mounted) and there was another devaluation in 1970. By that time, of course, import substitution had proceeded further as auto assembly factories, tire factories, chemical industries, and other new industrial enterprises had been established.

After the 1970 devaluation, foreign exchange receipts increased dramatically and growth was rapid over the next several years, although inflation accelerated and the exchange rate remained fixed in nominal terms. The fundamental strategy of growth through import substitution was unaltered.

After the oil price increase in 1973, the Turkish government kept the domestic price of oil constant, despite the country's total dependence on oil imports. Simultaneously, inflation accelerated sharply, reaching triple digits by the end of the 1970s. Nonetheless, the exchange rate was adjusted only after

13 See Anne O. Krueger, *Foreign Trade Regimes and Economic Development; Turkey*, Columbia University Press (New York), 1974.

considerable lags. The result was considerable overvaluation of the Turkish lira, and with it falling export earnings. By 1978 and 1979 growth of real GNP was estimated to be negative, excess demand for imports had reached major proportions, and the shortage of imports and foreign exchange was felt as the hard winter of 1979–80 came on: supplies of heating fuels were erratic and gasoline was in very short supply.

As table 3.2 shows, by 1980, Turkish per capita income was about the same as that of Korea. From table 3.4, Turkish exports were $2.9 billion, compared to Korea's $17.5 billion. No one could doubt that whereas Turkey's living standards, savings rate, and other indicators of economic performance were more satisfactory than Korea's in 1955, Korea's indicators were superior by 1980.

In 1977 and 1978, two devaluations and stabilization programs were announced and inaugurated. However, in each instance the program failed as devaluation lagged behind the rate of domestic price increase, and the government was unable to meet the targets set forth in letters of intent. Consequently, inflation continued to accelerate, and the overall economic situation deteriorated further. As in earlier periods, delays in receipt of import licenses increased, arrears in servicing debt mounted, and economic disruptions resulting from import shortages and other factors intensified.[14]

Finally, in January 1980, a major reform program was

14 There were major political difficulties in Turkey during this period, which in large part accounted for the government's inability to take more decisive action before 1980. In addition to import shortages and inflation, frequent strikes were an important source of difficulties. For an analysis of the political and economic factors leading up to the 1980 reforms, see Anne O. Krueger and Ilter Turan, "The Political Economy of Policy Reform in Turkey," in Robert H. Bates and Anne O. Krueger (eds), *Political and Economic Interactions in Economic Policy Reform Programs: Evidence from Eight Countries*, Basil Blackwell (Oxford), forthcoming.

announced. Unlike the 1958, 1970, 1977, and 1978 programs, the 1980 program had two objectives. In addition to stabilization, the intention to shift the economy from its import-substitution orientation toward a more outer-oriented, export stance and to increase reliance on the private sector for manufacturing and other productive activities, leaving the government to develop infrastructure, was stated from the outset of the reforms.

The initial devaluation (and increase in the prices of parastatal enterprise products) was accompanied by a sharp reduction in the magnitude of the fiscal deficit, which brought inflation down from an annual rate in excess of 100 percent at the time of devaluation to an annual rate of about 25 percent two years later. Subsequently, however, fiscal deficits have increased in magnitude, and the inflation problem in Turkey has not yet been satisfactorily resolved. Turkish debt-servicing obligations were a major problem in 1980, but they were rescheduled later on in that year, and Turkey managed to maintain creditworthiness throughout the 1980s despite her large debt-servicing obligations.

Incentives for tradable production and sale were altered beginning in January 1980, and further reforms were then undertaken over time. There was, of course, a sharp devaluation in January 1980, which itself significantly altered incentives. After several discrete devaluations to keep pace with inflation, in May 1981 it was announced that the exchange rate would henceforth be altered at very frequent intervals in order to maintain its real value in foreign currency. Thereafter, the real exchange rate for exporters was in fact made even more attractive, as changes in the nominal rate outpaced the differential in inflation rates between Turkey and her major trading partners.

Export incentives were adopted which were fairly uniform for all nontraditional export categories. Simultaneously, a series of measures were undertaken so that, by the mid 1980s, few quantitative restrictions on imports remained. Tariff rates were also gradually reduced after 1983. Restrictions on capital account were relaxed, as Turkish citizens became entitled to purchase larger quantities of foreign exchange for overseas travel, and businessmen could buy and sell foreign exchange for business purposes with few limitations.

Domestic financial markets were liberalized as the nominal rate of interest was set at levels above the rate of inflation, the Istanbul stock market was reopened, trading in foreign exchange was permitted, and holding of funds overseas was permitted. By the end of the 1980s, there were few remaining restrictions on the Turkish financial markets.

The policy reforms in Turkey have continued fairly steadily to the present time. Already, the structure of the Turkish economy has been transformed, virtually beyond recognition. Table 3.5 provides some indications of the results. Exports, which constituted about 5 percent of GNP in the late 1970s, were 20 percent of GNP by 1987. Exports grew at an average annual rate in excess of 20 percent throughout the decade, although their growth fell off sharply in 1989. Real GNP, which had been declining in the late 1970s, increased gradually – at rates above the rate of population growth – in the early 1980s. By 1985, however, growth was accelerating rapidly, and averaged more than 6 percent annually over the 1985–90 period.

The Turkish economy still has a number of structural problems, including inflationary pressures, as can be seen from table 3.5. However, most observers credit the reforms with a major structural transformation of the economy, and believe that, even if there is a future macroeconomic crisis, the shift toward a more outer-oriented and highly productive structure of economic activity will persist.

The Turkish reforms have already yielded a sizeable payoff, although a number of economic difficulties remain. A precise assessment would, of course, require specification of what would have happened in the absence of policy reforms. But, because of the size of payments arrears and other unsustainable elements of policy, it is not clear what the counterfactual alternative would have been. If successive Turkish governments had attempted to continue the policies of the late

Table 3.5. Turkish Economic Policies and Performance, 1978 to 1988

Year	Fiscal Deficit (% GNP)	Real Exchange Rate (1980 = 100)	Rate of Inflation (%)	Current Account (% GNP)	Export Earnings ($ million)	Growth of Real GNP (1980 prices)
1978	-3.9	83.4	45.3	-2.4	2,288	-2.9
1979	-5.4	75.4	58.7	-2.0	2,261	-2.6
1980	-3.5	100.0	110.2	-6.0	2,910	-1.0
1981	-1.7	117.0	36.6	-3.3	4,703	4.1
1982	n.a.	133.0	30.8	-1.8	5,746	4.5
1983	-4.2	142.2	31.4	-3.7	5,728	3.4
1984	-10.0	159.7	48.4	-2.8	7,134	6.0
1985	-7.4	156.1	45.0	-2.0	7,958	5.1
1986	-3.2	145.5	34.6	-2.6	7,466	8.1
1987	-4.0	136.6	38.8	-1.2	10,190	7.4
1988	-3.9	134.4	75.4	2.3	11,662	3.4

n.a. Not available.
Source: International Monetary Fund, International Financial Statistics Yearbook, 1990.

1970s, it seems clear that real output would have continued to fall, and inflation would have accelerated further. Contrasted with a scenario such as that, the Turkish reforms must be judged already to have been reasonably successful.

Argentina

By contrast with Korea and Turkey, a number of other countries have experienced severe economic difficulties and announced reform programs, only to find that after a short period of time, the same difficulties reemerged, or even intensified. The number of World Bank and IMF programs undertaken in each year of the 1980s (see table 2.1) is itself testimony to the continuation of the crisis.

For purposes of illustrating failure, a brief description of one such country is enough. Argentina is one country where several reform programs have been announced, many with great optimism.

Economic historians debate whether Australia or Argentina had the highest per capita income in the world in the late nineteenth century. Argentina's agriculture was highly productive and her infrastructure was excellent. The high standard of living was based largely on Argentina's exercise of her comparative advantage in exporting agricultural products. Until the 1940s, Argentina's history was also one of price stability, unlike some other Latin American countries.

As a result of these factors, even at the end of the Second World War, Argentina was more often regarded as a developed country than as a developing country. However, the Peron government which had come to power wanted to encourage domestic industry. Domestic prices of beef were suppressed to favor urban workers, and beef exports began declining in the 1950s. The internal terms of trade in Argentina were turned strongly against agriculture in an effort to encourage domestic industrialization and to favor urban workers.[15]

15 See Carlos Diaz Alejandro, *Essays on the History of the Argentine Republic*, Yale University Press (New Haven), 1970.

Simultaneously, public sector expenditures grew rapidly as workforces on the Argentina railroads, public utilities, and other publicly operated activities expanded and as governmental activities increased. Tax revenues, however, grew more slowly, with the result that sizeable public sector deficits emerged. The inevitable result was inflation, which on several occasions reached alarming rates.

For present purposes, it suffices to start with 1976, although there had already been several Fund stabilization programs, accompanied by debt-reschedulings, in earlier years. By 1976, inflation had accelerated and reached an annual rate of 500 percent. A military government assumed power and appointed a new economics team. That team, committed to bring inflation under control, announced a five-year program of tariff cuts, and took the usual stabilization measures. When, a year and a half later, inflation was still averaging 150 percent annually, it was decided that further measures were necessary.

The Argentine authorities thereupon announced the prefix of the exchange rate, setting a schedule by which the exchange rate would be altered. This was done on the theory that domestic prices would have to converge toward international prices under these circumstances.[16]

However, in the short run, the rate of nominal devaluation fell considerably below the rate of inflation. Simultaneously, the authorities had raised domestic nominal interest rates to make them positive in real terms, and they guaranteed foreign deposits of over one year. Foreigners were therefore provided with an opportunity to obtain a nominal interest rate reflecting Argentine inflation, but with a guaranteed conversion into dollars at the tablita-established rate. The

16 A five-year schedule of tariff cuts was also announced, and the first several tranches of cuts were made. However, there was so much water in the tariff that there was little reduction in the differentials between domestic and foreign prices resulting. Before the last scheduled cuts could be effected, balance of payments difficulties had reemerged.

real interest rate accruing to dollar depositers in Buenos Aires was therefore very high, and foreign deposits were naturally attracted.

However, as nominal devaluations of about 3 percent a month less than the rate of inflation proceeded, incentives for exports were reduced, and imports began flooding the domestic market. As observers noted the size of the emerging current account deficit, capital flight began, and dollar holders were no longer tempted by Argentine interest rates. The result was the end of that reform effort, as the authorities could no longer support the exchange rate to which they had precommitted. Fundamentally, the Argentina government had not reduced the size of its fiscal deficit sufficiently to reduce inflation below the 150 percent annual rate. Only in 1980 – when the prefix was in effect – did inflation fall to a double-digit rate. However, the government's overall deficit in that year was equal to 10 percent of GNP.[17] In 1981, the inflation rate again exceeded 100 percent, and it accelerated thereafter, reaching a rate of 662 percent in 1985.

By that time, the Argentine economy was once again in serious economic difficulties, as debt-servicing problems and mounting demand for imports in the face of declining foreign exchange earnings compounded the accelerating rate of inflation. The subsequent announcement of the "austral plan" was widely hailed as a bold and promising policy reform program. Under that plan, price controls were put into effect in addition to the other "usual" measures of an IMF stabilization program. The austral plan was initially regarded as a great success, as it was followed by a period of greatly reduced inflation (while price controls were in effect); from

17 *Economist*, January 26, 1980, Argentine survey, p. 19. A substantial fraction of the public sector deficit originated from defense spending and other components of the budget which were off-limits to the civilian economics team.

an annual rate of 662 percent in 1985, the recorded rate of inflation did indeed fall sharply, registering "only" 64 percent in 1986.

However, the underlying sources of inflationary pressure had not been adequately addressed. As price controls continued in effect, shortages intensified and black markets sprang up. Finally, price controls became ineffective and inflation accelerated to even higher rates than had previously been observed. Therefore, several other plans were put into effect, each with less short-term impact (because of a lack of credibility) than the preceding one, and, of course, no long-run impact.

President Alfonsin left office in the summer of 1989 before his term in office was to expire, as the monthly inflation rate reached 200 percent and food riots were taking place throughout the nation. Real GDP was estimated to be about 7 percent below its 1980 level, which implies a drop in per capita income of about 15 percent.[18] The foreign exchange situation was difficult, as Argentina had suspended interest payments on her $62 billion foreign debt in mid 1988. By December 1989, the austral stood at 5,000 per US dollar, compared to 10 per dollar two years earlier. A January 1990 scheme to reduce inflation witnessed a freeze on cash circulation (as holders of seven-day austral deposits were given ten-year dollar-denominated bonds to replace them), and inflation did in fact decline. By May 1990, the IMF released a stand-by which had earlier been suspended.[19]

However, although fiscal cuts were announced, they were not fully carried out. There followed renewed inflationary bursts, followed by new "austerity plans." Despite these, the 1991 inflation rate was 1,344 percent, and at the beginning of 1991, inflation was 37 percent at a *monthly* rate.

In February 1991, yet another economics team was

18 International Monetary Fund, *International Financial Statistics Yearbook*, 1990, Argentina pages.
19 *Financial Times*, July 12, 1990, p. 11.

appointed by the President, and Domingo Cavallo was appointed Economy Minister. He announced that his top priority was tax reform, although it could not be dealt with by Parliament until April, and anticipated opposition was substantial. Within several days of his appointment, two wildcat strikes were underway as workers were protesting Cavallo's first moves. A foreign diplomat commented, "Argentina has been sruggling with this same problem for years but just can't seem to deal with it."[20] The latest reported rate of inflation was for March 1991 – 95.5 percent, equal to 3,000 percent annually.

For present purposes, the point is that all Argentine policy reform programs have failed to address the major underlying issues of fiscal deficits, heavy protection of import-competing industries, and large inefficient public sector enterprises. In 1986, it was estimated that more than 85 percent of the country's fiscal deficit, which was 8–10 percent of GNP, was accounted for by the deficits of public sector enterprises. Since these agencies have not yet been successfully restructured, it has not been possible to do more than to provide breathing space through announced policy reforms which have consisted of price controls and other measures; the underlying sources of fiscal imbalance have not been addressed.

Interestingly, Argentina has received the support of the international institutions for each of these half-hearted efforts to slow down inflation. In one instance, the American government undercut the IMF team that was attempting to negotiate more meaningful ceilings and measures than the Argentine authorities were willing to undertake. A bridging loan from the US, combined with heavy pressure on the

20 *Financial Times*, February 7, 1991, p. 5, and February 8, p. 4.

World Bank to lend, effectively resulted in the inability of the IMF to influence economic policy sufficiently to make a real difference.[21]

Each Argentine reform has been launched with announcements telling of the great shift in economic policies, and the wonderful results that may be expected. In November 1990, for example, the *Financial Times* reported that "President Carlos Menem's tough economic adjustment policies have begun to bear fruit."[22] When that program had collapsed three months later and Cavallo was appointed Economy Minister, the *New York Times* headline read: "Renewed Optimism in Argentina."[23] It would hardly be surprising if Argentine citizens and foreign observers become increasingly skeptical of new announcements and new reform programs.

For purposes of these lectures, there are several points to be made. First, the payoff for successful and enduring reforms can be enormous. Second, the support of the international institutions and the international community has been virtually indiscriminately extended to far-reaching reform programs, such as the Korean and Turkish in 1980, and to ameliorative efforts to restore the status quo ante. There appears to have been an inability to differentiate sufficiently between the temporizing measures of countries such as Argentina on the one hand, and the more fundamental and far-reaching reforms of countries such as Turkey after 1980 on the other. What is needed is a more sophisticated appreciation of the differences between temporizing palliative programs, on the one hand, and genuine reform efforts, on

21 See David Finch, "Let the IMF be the IMF," *The International Economy*, Volume 2, No. 1, January–February, 1988, pp. 126–8. See also the *New York Times*, March 7, 1988, p. C2.
22 November 7, 1990, p. 6.
23 *New York Times*, January 31, 1991, p. C1.

the other. That, in turn, requires increased understanding and quantification of policies and their effects, a topic I shall return to in section 3.

2 Why Do Governments Adopt Policies so Inimical to Growth?

In the preceding discussion, I have assumed that the choice of economic policies is an exogenous event. Yet that leaves a problem: why do governments adopt policies that are manifestly inconsistent with growth? If alternative policies offer such a high long-run payoff, what is there in the structure of decision making that has led to such unfortunate choices? And why, when policy reform programs are undertaken, are they so often failures?

Given the evidence that alternative policies do in fact provide superior economic performance, the question assumes great importance. Research into this question has begun, and some parts of an answer are beginning to emerge, although important puzzles still remain, and increased understanding of the set of issues related to the determination of economic policies is an important item on the agenda of urgent research issues related to policy reform. Here, all that can be done is to sketch some of the insights that are beginning to emerge from consideration of political-economic interactions in developing countries.[24]

It has always been recognized that reforms may be politically difficult to put into place, and that there may be a period of time before the benefits begin to be felt. In part, political difficulty has arisen when reform programs have been poorly designed, so that short-term costs of adjustment have been greater than necessary. This was certainly the

24 See Anne O. Krueger, *Political Economy of Economic Policy in Developing Countries*, MIT Press, (Cambridge, MA) forthcoming, for a more extensive analysis.

case, for example, in Chile, in the early 1980s, when an inappropriate exchange rate policy sharply intensified economic difficulties. And, there is no question but that the failed reform programs of Argentina, Brazil, and many other countries have imposed real economic costs on many groups in society while failing to make a difference to longer-run growth prospects. In those circumstances, it is small wonder that new reform efforts encounter resistance from many groups in society.

However, there is more to the analysis of the political economy of reform than resistance during the transition period. Any analysis of the political economy of economic policy determination must be divided into two parts: those factors leading to the initial policy choice, and those tending to perpetuate the policy stance once it is effected. While there are clearly overlaps between the two issues, they are not in fact the same thing.

Turning first to the factors influencing initial choices, there are several components. It must be recalled that many of the developing countries achieved their independence from a colonial power in the postwar period, when their developmental efforts began, and when they were deciding upon the institutional structure and policies that were to be adopted for economic development. In that environment, it was perhaps natural to reject an open trade regime as a tool of colonial rule. But there were other important components. It will be recalled that the Great Depression had led to an abandonment of the belief in the functioning of markets in many quarters. Also, the legacy of the Russian revolution and the then-belief that the Soviet Union had achieved rapid growth through a centrally planned economy were also influential. In addition, examination of the very low per capita incomes in newly independent developing countries seemed to provide further evidence of market failure: not only was there an infant industry case, and the apparent example of the Soviet Union: it seemed self-evident that if markets had functioned properly, standards of living in the developing countries would be considerably higher.

A final factor underpinning the choice of development policy was that the idea of a "planned economy" was consistent with economic thought at the time. It was thought that there was little difference between government and private ownership, and that government officials could correct market failures and take into account differences between private and social profitability.[25]

Thus, the current state of economic thinking was not inconsistent with government ownership, intervention, and controls. In addition, however, there was an important underlying implicit political premise. That is, there was an implicit belief among economists that government was, or would behave as, a benevolent guardian in the Platonic tradition. It was assumed that politicians and bureaucrats would serve disinterestedly, calculating Benthamite social welfare functions, identifying market failures, and letting governments costlessly and flawlessly undertake functions to offset market failures. The idea that there might be government failure was seldom voiced. Indeed, Oskar Lange had, in 1940, provided a demonstration that was widely accepted that it was a matter of indifference whether governments or markets carried out production activities: central planners could provide appropriate signals to individual enterprise managers to achieve exactly the same results as would an ideal market mechanism.

This belief underlay most economists' discussions of economic policy in developing countries in the quarter century after 1945. The conditions under which perfect competition would provide a Pareto-optimal outcome were set forth; it was generally asserted that when these (very strict) conditions failed to hold, there was a case for government intervention. To add to the plausibility of the case for government intervention, the "infant industry" argument had long since

25 See Anne O. Krueger, "Ideas underlying Early Development Policy," paper prepared for Institute for Policy Reform, March 1991.

been recognized as an instance where market failure might be quite plausible. The fact that Alexander Hamilton had advocated it, and that the United States had imposed tariffs on some industries in the late nineteenth century was interpreted to support the view that the United States had grown *because* of tariffs.

With hindsight, some of the arguments advanced for intervention seem ludicrous: for example, it was argued that the state had to intervene to increase savings because the government would care more for the welfare of future generations than would private citizens. Thus, taxation for purposes of increasing savings was deemed a priority issue for governments.[26] What has since been learned is that politicians are far more concerned with the next election than are private citizens: if anything, the relevant discount rate in the political arena is higher than that in the marketplace!

In that intellectual atmosphere, it is certainly understandable that policies of "import-substitution" and of government production in parastatal enterprises, and the substitution of state agencies for private traders, bankers, and other economic agents, were undertaken. The emotional predisposition of the body politic in newly independent countries was favorable to rejection of a market solution, and economic theory seemed to provide a rationale for these departures.

Those factors, however, do not explain why government policies and enterprises so inimical to rapid economic growth persisted for so long. Here, the answer cannot be ideology and misguided economic analysis. It rests primarily elsewhere, although it must be emphasized that if research results had been sufficient to demonstrate the greater efficacy of alternative policy solutions, the ability of politicians and others to support the perpetuation of growth-inhibiting policies would have been substantially diminished. Until at least the 1980s, the ideology of import-substituting

26 Any of the early Indian five-year plans may be consulted for articulate expositions of this view.

industrialization was widely accepted and certainly provided a basis on which politicians and others could achieve popular acquiescence, if not support, for their policies.

But if ideology was a "permissive" factor, it was not a sufficient factor. First and foremost, once policies had been put in place and new institutions (or bureaucratic agencies) established to administer them, those administering the agency became a force in support of the perpetuation of the institution and its particular set of controls and regulations over economic activity. In many instances also, politicians perceived existing and new agencies as instruments with which to gain political support. Agricultural marketing boards, for example, which had been established under colonial rule as an instrument to aid farmers, were transformed first into institutions which could generate revenue for development efforts. Soon, however, those same marketing boards became convenient places for politicians to create employment for those whose favor they needed. As that happened, costs of marketing boards rose, the revenues which could be appropriated by the state fell, and the original and secondary rationales for the marketing boards were lost. However, in the process, reasonably strong vested interests had been developed which would make any effort to dismantle the boards and to trim their costs politically very difficult.[27]

This general pattern was repeated many times. An institution was established, often with idealistic, "paternalistic guardian" intentions. Over time, budgetary needs constrained its operations in one direction, while political pressures and uses of the agency increased its costs and the political support for the agency, driving it in the opposite direction.

In the case of agricultural marketing boards, support for

27 See for example, Anne O. Krueger, *A Synthesis of the Political Economy in Developing Countries*, *The Political Economy of Agricultural Pricing Policy*, Volume 5 of Anne O. Krueger, Maurice Schiff, and Alberto Valdés (eds). Johns Hopkins University Press (Baltimore), forthcoming.

perpetuation of the agency arose from politicians, bureaucrats, employees of the agencies, and sometimes from urban consumers, although budgetary pressures generally resulted in smaller consumer subsidies than is widely believed. Once these activities were undertaken, technical demands of economic activities were often beyond the scope of the agencies charged with them. Storage facilities were not available; purchasing agents did not arrive in rural areas in time to collect the harvest; or central points to which farmers were supposed to deliver their crops were far away from farms and there was no transport.[28] And, while the boards were failing in their assigned tasks, political constituencies resisting their abandonment mounted. Interestingly, there was seldom opposition to establishing new agencies to assume the functions the former agency had failed to perform, so the political response to complaints by farmers was often to "reorganize" the marketing functions by increasing the number of agencies and the number of persons employed by them. Thus, while economic results would have led to the abandonment of marketing boards, political support for them increased.

For other growth-inhibiting policies, other sources of support arose. In the case of heavily protected import-substitution industries, support came from domestic industrialists and labor unions, as well as bureaucrats in charge of administering licensing systems and controls. In the case of parastatal enterprises, it was evident that there would be major political resistance to laying off workers; indeed, in some instances, these institutions were deliberately used to absorb all college graduates seeking employment; as such, efforts to contain costs were futile.

Moreover, for many public sector enterprises, especially in

28 For an interesting account of some of the technical difficulties experienced in one country, see Nimal Fernando, "The Political Economy of Mahaweli," mimeo, World Bank Comparative Study on Agricultural Pricing Policies, 1987.

power, communications, and transport, rising costs were not immediately offset with increases in prices. This was part of the reason for the budgetary deficits, discussed earlier. But, once costs were significantly higher than prices, resistance to price increases intensified, both because users of these services believed themselves to be disadvantaged, and because of fears of the inflationary impact of any such changes.

There were, thus, a large number of political pressures that arose from the existence and operation of controls over economic activity that were created by the economic policies themselves. These pressures increased resistance to larger changes in the direction needed. To a degree, the ideology of development in its early decades led to wishful thinking: a public sector enterprise that was seen to be performing badly was reorganized; controls over the private sector were intensified in response to perceptions of the emergence of black markets or the failure of controls to achieve their stated purposes. A failed control was far more often replaced with a more complex set of controls or with an alternative administrative apparatus for its implementation than it was abandoned.

Once an institution or activity is in place, those who would lose by its elimination know who they are and can readily organize to oppose the change. Those who would gain do not know who they are. Not only can the former group organize more readily, public sympathy and support goes to those with whom there is a basis for identification. The identityless individuals who would be employed in new export industries, or who would otherwise be major gainers, are not known to individual citizens with the same concreteness as are the employees of particular enterprises, or civil servants. I have elsewhere described this phenomenon as "identity bias," which can affect the political pressures arising with regard to any economic reforms.[29]

29 See Anne O. Krueger "Asymmetries between Exportable and Import-Competing Industries," in Ronald W. Jones and Anne O.

However, economic phenomena impact on political events, just as political pressures influence economic policy decisions. In the case of interventionist controls, budgetary pressures resulting in inflation and excess costs led to low rates of economic growth and current account deficits. These economic pressures for change usually led to the economic crises that precipitated reform programs, as earlier discussed.

In a few instances prior to the late 1980s, the voters rejected excessive control mechanisms, or chose governments that would institute or perpetuate economic reforms. This happened in Sri Lanka in 1977, in Turkey in 1983, and in New Zealand in 1987, to name just a few instances. But, in the majority of cases, it was the direct pressures emanating from economic reactions to political events that resulted in policy changes.

It is an interesting question as to whether the events currently taking place in Eastern Europe will alter the thinking of citizens of other countries enough to change the political calculus as to the costs and benefits of undertaking far-reaching reform programs. Heretofore, politicians have been able to appeal to citizen support for "nationalistic" economic programs of the sort that have been inimical to growth. Should voters increase their awareness of the economic costs of controls, the political costs of resisting change will increase sharply.

Future Research Priorities

Increased awareness can, of course, come about through mechanisms other than the example of Eastern Europe. Indeed, as I already argued, the state of economic knowledge in the 1950s provided support for many of the policies that have, in practice, proved growth-inhibiting. To the extent that research can increase the economics profession's unanimity as

Krueger (eds), *The Political Economy of International Trade*, Basil Blackwell (Oxford), 1990.

to the costs of interventionist policies, it, too, will contribute to more rapid and more far-reaching alterations in economic policy. For that reason, I now turn to the final topic I wish to address.

That is, the need for additional research on the effects of alternative policies. The questions are interesting in themselves. They also have important implications for the future course of a great many countries both because there is need to know "how much is enough" regarding reform efforts, and because increased understanding will alter ideological and other resistances to policy reform. I have already sketched the outlines of a picture that is beginning to emerge with regard to the politial economy of policy formulation and policy change in developing countries. Clearly, that research must focus on interactions between economic and political variables and their evolution over time.

However, considerable additional research needs to be done. Many researchers, only a few of whom have been referenced, have attempted cross-country estimates of the relationship between domestic economic policies and various indicators of economic performance. A major difficulty has been that we lack systematic quantification, and, on occasion, even concepts with such quantification could be attempted, of major policies. Simon Kuznets was a pioneer in providing estimates of the way in which economies change during economic growth. His fundamental work permitted the analysis of a large number of issues in developing countries, which in turn increased our understanding of the development process enormously.

It is perhaps fitting, therefore, to close these lectures in his honor with a plea for efforts to find a conceptual framework with which to quantify various policies, and thus to build a better understanding of their individual (negative and positive) contributions to growth, and also to their interactions. International trade economists have been able to provide a conceptual basis on which the restrictist content of alternative trade regimes, and their average bias toward import-competing or exportable goods, may be quantified. To obtain the data is a tedious task, but it has been done and it has increased understanding of trade and payments regimes. The same sorts of efforts are inherently more difficult for domestic markets where border prices cannot serve as a frame of reference. Yet, a quantitative assessment of phenomena such as the real rates of return on public sector investments, the costs and benefits of maintenance programs, the value and cost effectiveness of alternative transfer mechanisms, and lowered productivity because of overinvestment and/or over-staffing of public sector enterprises is badly needed. We also need estimates of the impact on the price of labor of various governmental interventions, of the distortions in prices of credit generated by credit rationing, and of the quantitative magnitude of other governmental policies and controls which affect the incentives subject to which people make their decisions.

With estimates of those magnitudes, it should be possible to narrow the range of judgments about the impact of individual policies on growth performance, and to increase the confidence with which economists and policy makers can address policy reform issues. As that happens and, hopefully, as additional countries successfully reform their policies and embark upon rapid economic growth, one can hope that the learning process will enable other countries to undertake reform programs with greater confidence that the broad parameters are appropriate and that short-term costs are no larger than necessary. While judgments and political considerations will always be necessary in formulating and executing reform programs, it is to be hoped that increased understanding of the process will at least increase the probability of successful outcomes and the expected values of reform efforts.

Appendix: Policy Reform in Eastern Europe

In 1989–90, most Eastern European countries' policy makers began efforts to switch to a market economy after more than four decades of central planning.The necessity to undertake major changes in their economies was obvious: virtually all property was owned by the state; enterprises ordered their intermediate goods and raw materials in accordance with plans, and money was little more than a unit of account in those transactions; consumer prices were heavily subsidized; public sector deficits were substantial;. foreign trade was heavily oriented toward arrangements within the CMEA, and was conducted in inconvertible currencies, especially with the Soviet Union; and prices bore little, if any, relationship to costs.

To be sure, there were/are significant differences among the economies of the countries of Eastern Europe. Poland's agriculture had never been collectivized; Czechoslovakia had much less foreign debt and a much smaller "monetary over-hang" than did the other countries; Hungary had been under-taking reforms gradually since the 1970s and hence already had some relatively thriving private enterprises; Yugoslavia had had "labor-managed" enterprises and therefore had a different set of institutional arrangements governing enterprise behavior than did the other countries, and so on.

Nonetheless, the similarities among the Eastern European

countries was also striking. In every instance, fundamental changes had to be made in the ways in which decisions were made within enterprises; in the manner of doing business between enterprises; in the relationships between labor and management; in property rights; in foreign trade; and in the legal and institutional mechanisms governing resource allocation.

A systematic analysis of the problems facing the Eastern European countries in their process of reform would be a formidable task, requiring at least a monograph all of its own. An immediate and obvious question, however, is: What is the relevance of developing countries' experiences with policy reform for the Eastern European countries?

An effort to address that somewhat more limited question, at least briefly, is the subject of this appendix. A satisfactory answer even to that question cannot be given without a diagnosis of the problems confronting Eastern European governments in their efforts to switch to market economies.

Similarities and Differences between Eastern Europe and Developing Countries

A natural starting point, therefore, is an analysis of the similarities and differences between Eastern European countries' economies as of the late 1980s, and the "typical" middle-income developing countries as they embarked upon policy reform programs in the 1980s. Clearly, the situation was not the same in Eastern Europe as it was in Mexico in 1982, Argentina and Brazil in the late 1980s, or Turkey in 1980. The real question is how different it is, and what lessons apply.

Table A.1 provides some broad indicators of development status. As can be seen, the Eastern European countries had per capita incomes that were estimated to have been about the same as the per capita incomes of upper middle-income

Table A.1. Contrasts between Eastern European and Middle-income Developing Countries

	Per Capita Income, 1988 (US$)	Percent Enrolled in Secondary Education 1987	Life Expectancy 1988	Trade as % of GDP 1988
Bulgaria	2,027	n.a.	n.a.	63 (77)
Czechoslovakia	2,737	n.a.	n.a.	41 (77)
Hungary	2,460	70	70	38 (44)
Poland	1,860	80	72	27 (41)
Yugoslavia	2,520	80	72	38 (31)
Romania	1,482	79	70	43 (45)
Brazil	2,160	39	65	16
Mexico	1,760	53	69	27
Turkey	1,280	46	64	38
All middle-income developing countries	1,930	54	66	33

n.a. Not available.

Source: World Bank, *World Development Report*, 1990, for life expectancy and education for all countries and per capita incomes in Hungary, Poland, Yugoslavia and developing countries. Data reported in the *Financial Times*, August 15, 1990, p. 14 were used for per capita income estimates for Bulgaria, Czechoslovakia, and Romania. Those data, from other sources, provide much higher estimates of per capita income. The average differential between the estimates reported in the *Financial Times* and those reported by the World Bank for Hungary and Poland was used to deflate figures for the other three countries to a comparable basis. International Monetary Fund, *World Economic Outlook*, May 1990, p. 65 for data on trade (exports plus imports as a percent of GNP) for Eastern European countries. Data are for 1980. World Bank, *World Development Report*, 1990, for developing countries' trade. Figures in parentheses for Eastern Europe represent the fraction of total trade carried out with other east bloc countries.

developing countries.[1] Generally, they had a higher percentage of their GDP originating in industry, and a smaller percentage in agriculture, than did the middle-income developing countries.

Although per capita incomes do not appear to be greatly different, social indicators suggest somewhat greater well-being for the citizens of Eastern Europe. As can be seen from table A.1, reported life expectancies in Eastern Europe are above those of middle-income developing countries. Life expectancy in all middle-income developing countries in 1988 averaged 66 years whereas that in the high-income OECD countries averaged 76 years. The Eastern European countries were mostly halfway in-between, with life expectancies recorded at around 70 years of age. While life expectancy is not a perfect indicator of social well-being, there are reasons to believe that it reflects the provision of health care and basic nutrition reasonably well.

It is not really possible to contrast the roles of government in the economy. For one thing, state ownership of the means of production was pervasive in the Eastern European economies. A meaningful comparison would require evaluation of the percentage of private sector output in developing countries subject to government controls, if an effort was to be made to estimate the comparable importance of government in economic activity in developing countries. A second consideration is that prices were highly distorted in the Eastern European economies, with large subsidies to housing, trans-

---

1 All per capita income estimates are subject to considerable margins of error, especially when converted into US dollars. The reliability of the estimates is even more suspect when Eastern European data are used. On the one hand, most prices bear little relationship to international prices; moreover, they are often not even domestically market-clearing. On the other hand, complex systems of subsidies (as, for example, for housing) and failure to value services make estimates even more difficult. The data given in table A.1 are therefore indicative, at best, of broad orders of magnitude.

port, energy, and some other activities. This renders the use of budgetary accounts for purposes of comparison meaningless.

As can also be seen from table A.1, most of the Eastern European countries exported between a fifth and a quarter of their output. In that sense, they were "small, open economies," much like the middle-income developing countries. A major difference, however, was that almost all trade was state controlled, and the vast majority of transactions took place between the Eastern European countries and the Soviet Union, through the CMEA. In addition to other adjustments required in Eastern Europe, the shift away from dependence on CMEA trade and toward the international market increases the difficulties of the transition. Moreover, even those enterprises which had produced commodities for sale in the West were usually not subject to a meaningful budget constraint and had little idea of what their costs were.[2]

Published data suggest that most of the East European countries had higher savings rates than did the average of middle-income developing countries. While the usual caveats apply to direct comparison of data between market and non-market economies, the savings rate or a proportion of GDP

2 Ronald McKinnon has forcefully put forth the argument that many Eastern European enterprises were in fact producing "negative value added" at world prices. He argues that the heavy subsidies for energy and low prices for some materials relative to world prices meant that firms were using inputs to produce outputs that sold for less than could have been obtained by direct sale of the inputs. See his "Liberalizing Foreign Trade in a Socialist Economy: The Problem of Negative Value Added," paper presented at the Conference on Currency Convertibility in Eastern Europe, March 1991. Certainly, the evidence emerging from Eastern Germany is entirely consistent with this view. See George Akerlof, Andrew Rose, Janet Yellin, and Helga Hessinius, "East Germany in from the Cold: The Economic Aftermath of Currency Union," *Brookings Papers on Economic Activity*, Fall, 1991.

in 1988 for all middle-income developing countries averaged 27 percent. Yugoslavia's reported percentage was 40, Poland's 35, and Hungary's 268.[3]

In terms of assessing their potential for rapid growth, however, the biggest advantage of the Eastern European countries appears to lie in their greater stock of human capital. Most developing countries, as of the 1980s, had less well-educated populaces than did the Eastern European countries. The percentage of the eligible age group enrolled in secondary school in Eastern Europe was much higher than that in most middle-income developing countries.[4] In that regard, Eastern European countries appeared to be somewhat more "like" other European countries than like developing countries. Thus, in terms of starting income levels, social indicators, savings rates, and human capital stock, the Eastern European countries appear to have an advantage relative to most middle-income developing countries.

On the negative side, the Eastern European countries face challenges in creating institutions and incentives that will support the development of an economically efficient private sector. There is also a question, addressed briefly below, as to the value of their existing capital stock.

At first glance, this is the biggest disadvantage the Eastern European countries face as they attempt to transform their

---

3 Data from World Bank, *World Development Report*, 1990.
4 Most developing countries were able to increase the fraction of their populations enrolled in secondary education remarkably over the period after the Second World War, doubling on average the percentage enrolled in secondary school between 1965 and 1987. Most Eastern European countries had had much higher enrollment rates in the 1950s and 1960s. The differential in the fraction enrolled in secondary schools therefore greatly understates the great advantage the Eastern European countries have in their human capital stock. Interestingly, however, the fraction of the eligible age group enrolled in tertiary education was virtually the same in each of the Eastern European countries as it was for the average of all middle-income developing countries – 17 percent.

economies. Commercial codes, laws of contract, and well-established property rights did not exist and are prerequisites if there is to be any hope of developing a well-functioning market economy. There is little or no entrepreneurial tradition.

Establishing these basic institutions, and developing entrepreneurial traditions, cannot be done without "breaking" many existing relationships. For example, large-scale publicly owned enterprises have monopolies in the production of many commodities and intermediate goods.[5] Those using their products have received their inputs by dealing with the relevant ministry to which they reported. Not only must large-scale enterprises themselves be restructured in order to make them more responsive to incentives, but new relationships will be required between buyers and sellers, and firms using enterprises' products will themselves have to establish supply networks.

Starting Point for Reforms

As was seen in the second lecture, most developing countries have begun their reform programs under the pressures of high and accelerating inflation rates or of unmanageable debt-servicing obligations. These economic difficulties, in turn, have often resulted in relative unpopularity of the government at the outset of the reform process, and in little agreement upon the necessity for, or desirability of, policy reform. In addition, reforms meet opposition from the various interest groups that will stand to lose – protected firms producing import-competing products, public sector workers confronted with prospective layoffs or losses of jobs, consumers of subsidized foods, and so on.

By contrast, the momentum for policy reform in Eastern

---

5 They are also often vertically integrated, so that potential competition is foreclosed until they are broken up. Clearly, opening up the foreign trade regime is one means of providing competition, but problems nonetheless remain among domestic firms.

Europe appears to be generated largely by political considerations, and rejection of the earlier domination of the Soviet
Union. To that degree, reforms and changes in economic
policy contemplated in Eastern Europe bear a much closer
resemblance to the changes in economic policy that
developing countries undertook immediately after independence than they do to debt-crisis or inflation-induced reforms
in the developing countries in the 1980s. While there may
not be popular support for the precise content of reforms,
there does appear to be political support for policies which
break from the past.[6]

A second apparent advantage of the Eastern European
countries is that many of those with the strongest vested
interests in the old system – the bureaucrats and party officials
who were top enterprise managers – are politically weak, and
cannot exert political pressures through normal channels to
resist reforms. To be sure, appeal can be made to concerns
about enterprise closings, job losses, and other anticipated
and feared adjustment costs. But the individuals with most
to lose are politically weak relative to their positions in
developing countries when debt crises or inflation motivates
reform programs.

Overall, then, there is a certain political momentum, and
ability to innovate without the force of *directly* affected vested
interests in the Eastern European countries that is seldom
found in developing countries embarking upon reform programs. To that extent, reform should be easier in the Eastern
European countries.

There are also a number of similarities with policy reform
challenges in developing countries. In many of the Eastern
European countries, achieving macroeconomic stability (and

6 It has already been mentioned that the loss of CMEA trading
patterns provides something of a foreign trade crisis for most of the
Eastern European countries. To that extent, there is an economic
constraint that underlies reform efforts. Nonetheless, unlike the
situation in most developing countries, it must be judged that the
dominant impetus to reform is political.

especially freeing up domestic prices) is a major concern and involves reducing public sector deficits, just as in developing countries. As part of this process, a tax system must be developed virtually de novo, as the formerly used system of implicitly taxing enterprises and workers (by rationing commodities and hence preventing workers from spending their incomes) can no longer be used. In all of the Eastern European countries, reduction or elimination of subsidies and permitting prices to adjust to clear markets are essential components of reform efforts, both to attain macroeconomic stability and to achieve more efficient use of resources. Unrealistically low prices of energy and other material inputs have encouraged highly wasteful utilization, in addition to their budgetary implications. In addition, financial markets must be created, starting with a banking system, and extending through to stock markets and financial intermediaries of all sorts.

Finally, in all the Eastern European countries, reforms must be undertaken so that the foreign trade regime is relatively open and the exchange rate is realistic, providing adequate incentives for producers to seek export markets and signalling the relative scarcity of import goods.

In these dimensions, the initial conditions are little different from those of developing countries. The more striking difference, however, from that in developing countries is the necessity for the creation of laws and institutions which will provide adequate incentives for the rapid development of new earnings streams. While it is true that government ownership has been widespread in developing countries, and that government controls over prices, conditions of work, investment, and other aspects of private sector behavior have been a major determinant of profitability, property rights have been legally defined, laws of contract exist, and litigation procedures are in place. While, in some instances, these may be very weak,[7] they are nonetheless in place and do not usually require immediate attention as an important component of reforms.

7 See Hernando de Soto, *The Other Path*, Harper and Row (New York), 1989, for an exposition of the proposition that legal insti-

For the Eastern European countries, the issue of privatization of existing assets arises, and gets confounded with the issue of creating an appropriate institutional environment to provide incentives for, and legal protection of, new earnings streams, and the assets created by them.

The concern of policy makers in the Eastern European ▾ countries has naturally been focussed to a considerable degree on finding means for transforming the assets owned by the state into privately owned and managed properties. There are three general categories of assets that must be dealt with. First, there are relatively small enterprises and retail establishments, which appear to be relatively easily shifted to private hands.[8] Second, there is residential property, in which rights must be assigned. Here, earlier ownership claims and concerns about fairness both impede speedy resolution of the issue.[9]

The third issue pertains to large enterprises. Most industrial activity under communism was carried out in gigantic state enterprises; these enterprises are often monopolies, visible, and employ large numbers of workers. Many of them are of questionable efficiency. Issues in privatization arise both because many, if not all, components require major modification if they are to be commercially viable and because simply "privatizing" them does not remove monopoly power.

---

tutions and protection do not exist in the informal sector, and that their absence is a major source of low productivity in that sector.

8 See Stanley Fischer, "Privatization in Eastern European Transformation," paper presented at the Conference on The Transition to a Market Economy, Institutional Aspects, Prague, Czechoslovakia, March 1991.

9 Those who were highly placed in the earlier communist regimes typically are resident in the best dwelling units. A simple allocation of property rights to existing occupants would, many fear, reward a group that many believe have already fared very well. A possible solution would be to vest property rights in existing residents in all units deemed not to be significantly above "average," and to auction off the "top" units. Even then, there are concerns that the highest bidders will be those who profited most from the old regime.

That this will not be readily accomplished is evident both from the slow rate at which efforts to privatize have so far proceeded, and from the experience of the Treuhandanstalt, which has had considerable resources at its disposal in its effort to find new owners/managers for the large enterprises of the former German Democratic Republic.[10]

Agenda for Reform

The preceding discussion has already pinpointed the similarities and differences between policy reform in developing countries and those in Eastern Europe. Politically, Eastern European countries' citizens appear to be willing to sacrifice and to accept a period of stagnation to achieve the transition to a market economy, although it is clear that the longer the period of hesitation and failure of new earnings streams to be generated, the more frail will that support become.

Economically, Eastern Europe's great advantage relative to most middle-income developing countries is that there is a much better human capital base on which to build. This would suggest that, if appropriate reforms are undertaken, the world should witness the emergence of a group of exporters whose comparative advantage lies in heavily human capital, or skill-using, activities.

Those appear to be the large pluses. In many regards, there are strong similarities between the situation in developing countries and that in Eastern Europe. While it is true that much more of economic activity is already in private hands in most developing countries than was true in 1989 in Eastern Europe, it was largely governmental controls, permissions, and policies that determined profitability. A reorientation of habits of producers away from a focus on decisions in the

10 See Akerlof et al., "East Germany in from the Cold," for an account of the difficulties encountered by enterprises in Eastern Germany.

nation's capital and toward conditions in the national and international marketplace may be almost as difficult in developing countries as in Eastern Europe.

Clearly, the need to open up the Eastern European economies and to reorient trade with the international economy bears strong similarities to the problems confronted in developing countries where trade policies have been highly protectionist. Perhaps it will, in the long run, be an advantage for the Eastern European countries that the collapse of the CMEA arrangements will force that opening. There is, however, a risk that protection of domestic industries may initially be granted (for fear that too many jobs will initially be lost otherwise) and then become built into the structure of incentives.

In that regard, the Eastern European countries can learn a lesson from the post-independence experience of developing countries: while protection may initially be granted to domestic industries for reasons of high principle, those receiving the protection will rapidly organize into a politically effective group to support the maintenance of protection. Those contemplating protection as a solution to a short-run problem would be well advised to count, as one of the potential costs, the possibility (or probability) that, once in place, protection will be difficult, if not impossible to remove.

Governments in Eastern European countries also face much the same challenge as those in developing countries in removing controls over prices of goods and factors and in achieving reasonable macroeconomic stability. As already indicated, the challenge of developing new sources of government revenue is more pressing and more formidable, in that the former sources of revenue largely vanish immediately upon the shift away from a command economy.

The biggest issue, and the one that creates most difficulties for Eastern European countries, is the shift from government ownership to private ownership. That shift can, logically, be divided into two parts: the creation of an environment in which new earnings streams will rapidly emerge; and the assignment of property rights to existing physical assets.

The former task is by far the more important. Clearly, the economies of the Eastern European countries must be largely transformed, and it is the new earnings streams which will emerge that will permit rapid increases in productivity and living standards. Creation of that environment requires the establishment of some basic institutions which will provide secure property rights for those who undertake new activities, so that they have appropriate incentives and that they have secure claims to their earnings. Without these, it is unlikely that very many will be willing to accept the risks and challenges of responding to the altered incentive systems that reforms are designed to generate.

In addition to property rights, a commercial code, and a mechanism for enforcement of contracts, must be put into place. These, in turn, require the existence of an institution or institutions in which disagreements over property rights or between contracting parties may be adjudicated.

Getting a legal/institutional framework in place which protects those who create new earnings streams is perhaps the single most important task of reform in Eastern Europe that has no counterpart in developing countries. In principle, it should not be difficult to adopt, relatively swiftly, a commercial code and other necessary legal underpinnings from one of the Western European countries.

In practice, however, the issue of allocating property rights in existing assets has caught attention. Focus is upon the assignment of property rights of existing state-owned assets. In theory, as long as legal and institutional processes are in place for markets for new activities, the process of privatization of state-owned assets need not be swift. In practice, however, the issue of disposition of those assets has been confounded with the issues surrounding new earnings streams. For reasons already mentioned, there appears to be little difficulty with privatization of small-scale commercial activities. It is in the market for residential properties and large-scale enterprises that problems emerge.

The difficulties, both in assuring improved management,

and in attempting to achieve equity, are enormous.[11] How serious delays in completing the task are depends heavily on two things: the uncertainties created thereby; and the actual value of the earnings streams (evaluated at international market prices) that may be generated by these assets once they are privatized. To the extent that existing capacity is regarded as a potential source of supply, new entrants to these activities may be deterred.[12]

As of early 1991, there had been very little success with privatization of residential assets or of large state-owned enterprises in most of Eastern Europe. Clearly, the ability of Eastern European governments either to privatize more rapidly or to provide security for new activities insulated from uncertainties as to the disposition of the large industrial enterprises will be critical to the economic prospects of those countries.

It is in the critical dimension of creating institutions and incentives for private economic activity that the success or failure of Eastern European governments' reform programs will largely be determined. While developing countries such as Turkey and Mexico have needed to modify existing laws governing, e.g., foreign investment, these have not been essential as part of the initial group of policy measures, and they

11 See Jean Tirole, "Privatization in Eastern Europe," in National Bureau of Economic Research, *Macroeconomics Annual*, 1991, for an analysis of the issues that must be confronted in privatization of large-scale enterprises.

12 And, to the extent that state-owned firms are permitted to continue production while being subsidized by the state, the situation would be even worse: potentially viable producers may not enter because the pricing from state-owned enterprises is not reflective of costs; simultaneously, the deficits of the state-owned enterprises either crowd out other, more productive, public investments in infrastructure or they contribute to macroeconomic instability.

have been additions to an existing structure.[13] For Eastern European countries, establishing these institutions is essential before very much private economic activity can be expected to develop. And that is the dimension of policy reform in Eastern Europe which has no obvious counterpart in the reform programs in developing countries.

13 There are some countries in which the absence of clearly defined property rights, especially in land, is a significant deterrent to increased agricultural productivity. Even then, clarifying or creating property rights is normally undertaken over a longer period of time and is not part of an initial package of policy reforms.

Index

concept of 62–7
conditions under which it
was taken 81–8
evaluation of 76–8
identification 64
and international
institutions 117, 118
macroeconomic 93–102
need for 1, 59, 93, 97,
118, 168
in the 1980s 80–1
objective of 106, 113
programs 29, 94, 117, 120
and trade and payment
regime 92, 102–8
see also reform program
political infeasibility 61, 97
Prebisch, Raul 5 n., 41
pressure
bugetary 28, 156, 158
inflationary 91, 101, 105,
123
political 40, 119, 158, 159,
169
pressure group 104
pricing
agricultural 30, 34, 92
panterritorial 27
property rights 163, 167,
170, 171 n., 174, 176 n.
public sector 13, 20, 40
deficit 15, 16, 93, 94,
148 n; *see also* deficit,
fiscal
efficiency 98, 110
savings *see* savings
public sector enterprises 24,
28, 64, 109, 110 n; *see
also* state-owned
enterprises (SOEs)

quantitative restrictions 11,
66, 90 n., 103, 104, 105,
113, 115

rate of return
on private investments 98
on public sector
investment 98, 160
Rayner, Anthony 128
reform 2–3, 52
magnitude of 110, 111,
112
political economy of 125,
152
range of 111
speed of 111, 113
timing and sequences of
113
reform program 9, 59, 60,
61, 86, 91, 93–7, 111,
112
credibility of 94, 108,
112–13, 115
duration of 67–9
experience with 125
see also policy reform,
programs
regulations 36, 41
in factor markets 36–7
Reichmann, Thomas 76 n.,
80 n.
repression, financial 37 n.
Rodrik, Dani 106 n., 115 n.
Rose, Andrew 166 n.
Ruttan, Vernon W. 9 n.

Sachs, Jefferey 122, 128 n.
SAFs *see under* structural
adjustment
SALs *see under* structural
adjustment